KNIGHTS
of the Road

BY THE SAME AUTHOR

Congress Investigates:
A Documented History (with Arthur Schlesinger, Jr.)

Am I Not a Man and a Brother:
The Antislavery Crusade of Revolutionary America, 1688–1787

KNIGHTS
of the Road

A HOBO HISTORY

Roger A. Bruns

 METHUEN, NEW YORK

FOR
Carrie, Margaret, and Sharon

Library of Congress Cataloging in Publication Data
Bruns, Roger.
    Knights of the road.

    1. Tramps—United States—History.   I.   Title.
HV4504.B78   305.5′6   80-15661
ISBN 0-416-00721-X

Manufactured in the United States of America by
Fairfield Graphics, Fairfield, Pennsylvania
Designed by Helen Barrow

First Edition
Published in the United States of America by
Methuen, Inc.
733 Third Avenue
New York, N.Y. 10017

Acknowledgments

Numerous institutions and individuals gave generous assistance in the preparation of this volume. I would like to give special thanks to the Antiquarian & Landmarks Society of Connecticut, which holds the invaluable John J. McCook Collection. Arthur Leibundguth and Trudy Schobinger of the Society have been enormously supportive throughout the course of my work. Long live the Cat's Meow.

I am grateful to Mary Lynn McCree and Mary Lynn Ritzenthaler of the University of Illinois at Chicago Circle for their valuable assistance in working with the Ben Reitman Papers. These two individuals along with their assistants have made the manuscript division of this library one of the most professional and helpful I've seen.

I wish also to thank Adela Haberski French, the editor of the McCook microfilm guide, who shared many of her insights into the Reverend's work; Jay Facciolo and Mark Jury, who shared their ideas and work; Dan Preston, a superb researcher who helped uncover elusive hobo writings; George Vogt, Richard Sheldon, and Carrie Bruns, who critically read the manuscript; and Mary Giunta, Anne Henry, and Sara Jackson, who provided valuable leads to documents.

Finally, I would like to express my appreciation to the several men still on the road, especially Hobo Bill, the Cheyenne Kid, Mountain Dew, Frisco Jack, Sparky Smith, and Steam Train Maury Graham, who shared their stories and perceptions of the hobo life. Their words confirm the spirit that still lives, expressed by an old hobo named A. W. Dragstedt who wrote for a hobo newspaper in the twenties. Dragstedt called his fellow hoboes "pioneers": "I drive my pick into the sunbaked prairie ridges of Texas or the crawfish dirt from between the roots of the Pineries of Louisiana and Mississippi to build the roadbed, whereon will be stretched the ribbons of steel; or to spade in a barrowpit in an oozing muskeg swamp in Wisconsin; or to drive a drill into the mountains wherever it be. Only so that man may be able to distribute in more efficient ways the things people need—such as the grain I help to harvest in the scorching heat of summer by shocking the bouquets of wheat for the daily bread. Now do you know what the hobo is?"

Copyright Permissions

Contents

List of Illustrations

KNIGHTS
of the Road

1/ *An Endangered Species*

Few HOBO JUNGLES remain. The men and women, thousands in the early years, who passed through them—the working stiffs, gay cats, yeggs, and prushins—are now history and legend. The ones who try to carry on the life of the road are a vanishing species. "They're clearing out fast," laments the Cheyenne Kid, a soft-spoken veteran of the rails, "and I mean fast. We're a dying race." The Pennsylvania Kid agrees. Sporting a plumed headdress and a long coat covered with an assortment of buttons, the grizzled Kid, who insists he hasn't slept in a bed in fifty years, speaks wistfully of the glory days of hoboing when thousands of itinerant workers beat their way across a country laced with railroad lines, when the vagabond spirit was something to be respected and admired. Today, he says, the road has bums who won't work and winos who can't, but it has few hoboes.

It is August in Britt, Iowa. Each year, for half a century, hoboes have gathered in Britt for an annual "Hobo Convention" in this small farm community. The convention this year has drawn thousands of residents, visitors, political figures, and other curious onlookers; it has drawn only a few hoboes—Lord Open Road, the Cheyenne Kid, the Pennsylvania Kid, Frying Pan Jack, Steam Train Maury Graham, Frisco Jack, Virginia Slim, Rattlesnake Jack, and perhaps ten others. Here at the convention they renew acquaintances, make a few speeches, and elect a hobo "King" and "Queen." But mostly they sit and swap stories—of nights on the top deck, rolling across silent prairies; of nights precariously clinging to brake rods inches from biting, tattooing cinders, fighting off the force of the curves; of the sight of mangled comrades who had made the false step or the ill-timed leap or had fallen asleep at the wrong time; of the countless jobs, some good, some tolerable, many bad; of all the sights, from the main stem of West Madison Street in Chicago to the forests of the Northwest to the berry fields of California; of the hostile towns and bulls; of the times in jail and on chain gangs; of nights shivering on floors of cheap missions or huddled in boxcar corners; of the other 'boes, hundreds, all with their stories of survival; of the hunger, sometimes relieved by jungle feasts, sometimes by a mission's stale bread and watery soup; of the cat-and-mouse chases with railroad shacks; of the thundering beat of train wheels on the Sunshine Special, the Panama Limited, and the Yellow Dog; of adventure, freedom, and fear. In the corrugated faces of the 'boes are the strains and challenges of the road.

Frying Pan Jack has hoboed for more than fifty years, working for railroads, chopping wood, carrying trash—numberless jobs. His monicker suggests his special talent in the jungle. But it's all changed, he says. "We've got no good jungles left. Most of the old-timers are gone. The kids and I have nothing to talk about because we're three generations apart." Frying Pan has been running for the hoboes' highest office at Britt for several decades. "Herbert Hoover was running for President the year I left home. He won, but I never have."

Steam Train Maury Graham spent eight years on the road as a young man, got married, worked as a cement mason in Toledo, raised two daughters, and returned to the hobo life in 1968. A rough-hewn, white-maned, Santa Claus-like figure who leans on a curved walking stick, Steam Train is credited by some 'boes with discovering an infallible economic law. The United States economy, so the law asserts, can be measured by the length of cigarette butts: short butts mean adversity; long butts, prosperity. Steam Train, who still hops trains in the East, estimates that there are fewer than thirty genuine, train-jumping hoboes still traveling across the country. In his wanderings in the East, he never sees another fellow 'bo. Unquestionably the most recognized hobo in America, Maury seems to have friends everywhere. He speaks to school groups and visits veterans hospitals, penitentiaries, and retirement homes, telling the hobo story.

Steam Train and other nomads who still ride the freights remember fondly their famous departed rail heroes—the Hardrock Kid, Hairbreadth Harry, Scoopshovel Scotty, Roger Payne the Hobo Philosopher, Cannonball Eddie Baker, Jeff Davis, and the diminutive, dynamic Ben Benson. Bennie was an acknowledged lord of the rods for over forty years, as well as a poet and writer. His autobiography stands as a monument to self-glorification. When the Pennsylvania Kid looks back at the world's greatest men he sees a triumvirate—Jesus Christ, Socrates, and Ben Benson. Some of the comrades have only recently passed on. When he died at age eighty-five, Bigtown Gorman had never learned to drive a car. But he had seen more of the country than anyone, except other hoboes perhaps, had read two newspapers a day, and was a walking stock-market tote board. Bigtown was a scissors sharpener who claimed he worked on the most important scissors in the nation—Truman's, Eisenhower's, Kennedy's. He didn't want to sharpen Nixon's. In his last years, Bigtown had to give up the sharpening work. After he had a heart pacemaker implanted, the sharpener's electric motor once nearly killed the old 'bo by jamming the pacemaker circuits with static electricity.

As their numbers dwindle, as the once common sights of men clinging to freights and communing in the jungles near extinction, the survivors remain eager to tell the story, a story laden with contradiction and paradox. From the comic caricatures of Charlie Chaplin and Emmett Kelly to the image of brutal savagery painted by writers such as Robert

Penn Warren, the hobo figure has been one of contrasting symbols. He has stood as the frustrated western pioneer with too few lands to conquer. He has stood as the iconoclast, defying traditional values and custom, bent on staking his own claim to the American ideal of rugged individualism. He has been a testament to failure, wallowing in degradation, the polar opposite of the Protestant ethic of success through hard work. Idealistic dreamer—public dreg. To welfare agencies his numbers represented an insoluble problem. To many social reformers he was a tragic symbol of capitalistic exploitation. To American industry he and his labor were necessary evils. The story has many colors and sides. To Thomas Wolfe it was "a legend of pounding wheel and thrumming rod, of bloody brawl and brutal shambles, of immense and lonely skies, the savage wilderness, the wild, cruel and lonely distance of America."

The siren's call of the railroad gripped thousands in the late 1800s. By the end of the nineteenth century, the railroad's steel arms reached nearly every county in the United States, almost 200,000 miles of track. The railroad brought not only mobility but also romance. The wail of the soot-belching monster locomotives touched nerves of restlessness. One early hobo described its compelling, almost mystical attraction: "A train is a thing compounded of magic and beauty . . . the rattle and swank of a long freight pulling out of the yards, the locomotive, black and eager, shoving her snorting muzzle along the rails . . . is a spectacle and a challenge which only the wanderer who loves train riding can understand." The poet Harry Kemp, who had jumped many a freight, once wrote:

> Singing the song of their traffic
>   As they ride like ships in a gale:
> For ships in the wind lift music
>   Of a song that is all their own—

And, chanting down grooves of metal,
  To a modern symphony grown,
The rhythmic cars have voices
  That the man who rides them knows.

The Civil War had turned thousands of boys into disci-
plined foragers, resilient, hardened, able to find food and
shelter in all conditions, proficient in the use of the railroad.
After the war, many of these men, uprooted and inured to
years of wandering and fighting for survival, found peace an
unsettled time. Many had no homes or ties—or had forgotten them. Few jobs awaited. Now, with the days of troop
movements and army camp life and dodging hostile forces
behind, many continued their wandering—picking up odd
jobs, sleeping outdoors under any available cover, begging
meals, a new kind of adventure for which they were well
trained. They followed wagon roads and trails. But mostly
they hit the tracks.

And others were taking to the road. As machines in the
second half of the nineteenth century displaced numerous
workers in such industries as iron, coal, printing, and glass
and in shoe factories and flour mills, many workers sought
relief in other areas of the country. Industrial depression
brought migrants, and of those who chose the road to look
for employment, many never returned to a permanent job.

Some on the road were driven by wanderlust, an insatia-
ble drive to keep moving. Robert Service wrote of its power:

Haunting, taunting, that is the spell of it;
Mocking, baulking, that is the hell of it;
But I'll shoulder my pack in the morning, boys,
And I'm going because I must;
For it's so-long to all
When you answer the call
  Of the Wan-der lust.

Dan O'Brien, a road knight celebrity and philosopher in the
twenties and thirties, wrote of the hobo, "He is the man in

whom the wanderlust is the strongest lust ... reckless, perambulating soldier of fortune. ... Women and other trifling things don't bother him. ... He is an avowed optimist, laughs a great deal at the gyrations of men, looks upon politicians as tyrants, the clergy as supreme dodgers of things religious, hopes the human race, like whiskey, will improve with age."

The road became a melting pot for men who had been prosperous in business and who ran from failure or personal problems; men who had known nothing but poverty; men with no families; skilled mechanics who had lost themselves in booze; boys escaping from boredom; ex-railroad workers who had lost their jobs but not their attachment to the train; some immigrants who chose the open air of the Plains or the West to the stifling misery of a factory job and ghetto; men with criminal records and few places to go for work; men running from the police; grafters, gamblers, and thieves plying their trades. They all shared a common need: to quench a thirst for moving; to trust their fates to the whimsical notion that a better life lay somewhere down the track.

In this swelling cadre of wandering, homeless men were those that were to comprise an important labor force. The drive of American industry westward opened new kinds of jobs—at the railroad construction sites, in the mines, in the timberlands, on the sheep and cattle ranches, in the grain belt, in the orchards. The call was for a special kind of labor, a labor remote from family and community life. The jobs were irregular, in scattered and often isolated areas. The itinerant miners, loggers, bridge snakes, skinners, muckers, tunnel workers, and ice harvesters who answered the call were mobile and adaptable. When Steam Train Maury Graham and the Cheyenne Kid declare that hobo labor built much of the West, they are not exaggerating. From diamond cutting in the winter waters of Minnesota to railway construction in Utah, to felling timber in the Northwest, to working the mines in Montana, the boomer workers filled enormous labor needs.

In the boxcars or "side-door pullmans," on the open "gondolas," in the "death woods" (the plank above the coupling of boxcars), in the empty battery boxes, on the cowcatchers in front of the engines, in the animal cars, on the brake rods, even in the piles of coal in the coal cars, the workers crisscrossed the country, took odd jobs, worked for a spell, and then moved on. "When I was pulled through the door of the boxcar," one hobo wrote many decades ago, "I was pulled into another world, a world of adventure and hardship. . . . I felt that my past life had been shut out. I was no longer a plodding farmhand. I had stepped outside the law, into the realm where men lived by their wits. If we were caught it meant prison, but the idea filled me with an elation hard to describe." Another put it more directly, "It's just like taking marijuana. It's habit forming, it's a disease . . . you piss out a boxcar once, you're hooked."

A few women also challenged the freights. One hobo raconteur in the early years wrote about the story of "Boston Betty," a spirited sort who on one memorable day foiled all the best efforts of railroad shacks and bulls to keep her from holding down a freight over one particularly rough stretch of road. With the eagle-eyed train crew ready to intercept any dash Betty might make for the usual nests, the blinds or the vestibule steps, she ran down the track so fast that by the time the pilot was abreast of her the train was going too fast for the crew to bother stopping it. As the cowcatcher came even with her, Betty swung aboard and crawled onto the crosspiece about six inches from the rails. "She made it to the next station okay," the hobo storyteller concluded, "but the damn engine hit a cow before it got there, an' you should have seen Betty when she crawled off!" What did the storyteller think of all of this? "Tough on the cow!"

Frisco Jack, a veteran world-traveled 'bo, remembers hoboes barnacling themselves on the runway across the top of boxcars. On hot desert crossings, he says, some daring and desperate train jumpers would slide into the "reefers" (refrigerator cars), perch on top of the ice, and enjoy a cool excursion. Some, however, received the ultimate cold. "If a trainman came through and put a pin through that hasp, you'd be a trapped pigeon. They pulled many dead men out of those cars." A grisly end under the killer wheels awaited many jumpers. Legions of 'boes lost arms and legs. But the number of men on the road continued to grow.

To many Americans, the burgeoning hobo army was a teeming mass, foreboding, ominous, a collection of misfits and degenerates, parasites who survived by stealing, begging, marauding, and murdering. But the road thugs were not usually the workers, Frisco Jack explains. The jackrollers and thieves not only gave the hobo a bad name but preyed on him. Many a stiff returning from the timberlands or the wheat fields fell victim to those whose favorite sport was "harvesting the harvesters." Many 'boes lost more than their winter stakes to the yeggs. Numerous mutilated bodies found along the tracks were a gruesome testament to the violence of some of the road predators. "To the general public," Jack continues, "anybody that rode the freight train was to be despised. Maybe you'd ask for a glass of water and they'd slam the door in your face . . . many a time I wouldn't have the courage to ask them." Although the class distinctions were often blurred, although the hobo in times of trouble had to beg and panhandle and pilfer vegetables and other food to survive, he was willing to work.

Not so the tramp and bum. To outsiders the words *hobo*, *tramp*, and *bum* appeared synonymous. In the vernacular of the road, the distinctions were unmistakable and critical.

The men at Britt carefully point out, as did their forebears, that the hobo was a migratory worker, the tramp was a migratory nonworker, and the bum was a nonmigratory nonworker. Although the tramp roamed the country as arduously as the hobo, he was a professional idler, not a worker. To the tramp, the hobo's willingness to labor was a sorry capitulation to society's norms. The tramp credo was absolute aversion to work, the Protestant ethic upside down. Carl Sandburg, who spent many of his early years on the road, wrote that the tramp "can't even think about work . . . and it gives him a pain in the ass to talk about it." If most Americans regarded idleness as sin, the tramp worshiped it. "Work," a tramp once proclaimed, "has wasted more human life and happiness, and cemented the foundations of more inhuman wrong, oppression, and misery than ever did the combined energies of war, physics, and bad whiskey." The tramp was a scientist of survival, a master of begging, petty larceny, and con jobs. The bums were yet another story— the human wreckage along the skid road curbs, the men with upturned cups and downturned faces. The bums seldom left the haunts of the inner city. They were the dirt under society's totem pole.

But the hobo, the Pennsylvania Kid explains, was of a higher order than the tramps and bums. The hobo "never wanted anything for nothing." He was the working class of the road. Even Theodore Roosevelt was made aware of the crucial hierarchical standing. John Ellis, a prominent 'bo named the "apostle of the unemployed" after a hobo convention in 1907, managed to get an audience with the President, the Rough Rider who always fancied himself a man of the road and the wilds. Ellis carefully explained that the unemployed workers were not tramps and bums. "You may call them hoboes if you will," Ellis instructed, "but do not confound hoboes with tramps and bums."

The caste lines for some were constantly shifting with the eddies of economic and social forces. A man might have been a worker for a period of time, then live a tramplike existence for a while, and then return to seasonal occupations. Some might succumb to the ravages of alcohol or despair, give up the wandering, and hang around a city begging and mooching.

Several claims have been offered for the derivation of the word *hobo*. Some have insisted that the word comes from the Latin *homo bonus* or good man. Others have said that it was first used by soldiers returning home after the Civil War who, when asked where they were headed, would reply "*ho*meward *bo*und." Jeff Davis, longtime hobo king and showman, claimed that the word referred to "hoe boy," a term used in the eighteenth century for a migratory agricultural worker. Godfrey Irwin, an authority on tramp and criminal word etymology, talked to numerous hoboes early in the century attempting to find the origin of the word, but he also found no conclusive answers. Apparently the men themselves, in the 1890s, were not aware of the derivation. One veteran knight of the road asked numerous old hoboes how the word should be spelled, what it meant, and where it came from and received many conflicting and confusing replies. Frustrated, he gave up and began simply to use the French *haut beaux*, a more aristocratic appellation for his fraternal brethren.

If the origins of the word itself have eluded the hobo brotherhood, the men have had no question about the influence of their work. Ben Benson once declared that hoboes "are the REAL backbone of the Nation: the first to be called upon in time of war—and the last to be helped, as they should be in times of depression. . . . The hoboes ARE a respectable and necessary part of our population. THEY helped to MAKE this country! They helped to make it GREAT!" Resentful that society has mixed the road worker in the same social cauldron with common street dregs and thieves, hoboes declare that they and their fellow workers helped lay the railroads, drill the oil wells, fell the trees, dam the rivers, harvest the crops, and dig the mine shafts in raw virgin wilderness, the cutting edge of the frontier. The oil fields, construction sites, berry fields, logging camps, and canneries offered work that was long and hard and pay that was usually two weeks late. The "board and room" that went with the job was often lice-infested sleeping quarters and stomach-churning food. But they did the work and moved on.

Some hoboes drifted aimlessly in a devil-may-care series of hops from harvest field to harvest field, from construction job to construction job. Others, more cautious and calculating, plotted their seasonal wanderings more carefully. One might start in the oil fields, move to cotton and wheat harvests, railroad construction, and then cattle ranches; another might work the woods of the North for a few months, move to spring work on farms, county road work, and then to the Midwest harvests. But mostly the hobo moved to conflicting reports and rumors of better jobs on down the line. A short stay in California might bring a couple of weeks of pruning, a couple more of picking apricots. Rumors of jobs in Idaho mines could then stampede him along with hundreds of others. More nights on freights. When San Francisco advertised its Exposition, the westbound brake beams and top decks were clogged with eager stiffs and the city's charity organizations became hopelessly glutted with the disappointed unemployed.

Almost everywhere he traveled, the hobo faced competition for jobs from itinerant workers who were less mobile. Many mechanics living near the wheat belt, for example, worked the harvests each year. A hobo working the fruit orchards of California might labor side by side with hundreds

of pickers who had never left the state. But the farmers and
the mine operators and the railroad builders couldn't rely on
a meager supply of home-guard labor. The thousands of
workers of the road were crucial to these and other industries. One observer of the floating laborer noted in 1914,
"The day has gone when the American farm hand was a
stout young fellow who expected, after he had saved a little
money, to stake out a quarter section of his own. The quarter sections are all taken up. The farm hand is now a casual
laborer, working hard during the plowing and planting season, tramping or resting until harvest time, working at bo-
nanza wages for a few weeks during the harvest—and, when
that is done, living as best he can during the winter. Of like
habits are the men who construct the railroads, dig our irri-
gation ditches, cut our timber, load and unload our freight at
the lake ports." Boom and bust, explosion and implosion of
labor. Battalions of workers marched to the pulse of on-
again, off-again employment.

In tramp and hobo lore the first professional train-jumping men of the road were two discharged Union soldiers
who took the names "Erie Crip" and "Philly Pop." Their
monickers, like the thousands taken by stiffs through the
years, gave the road initiates new identity and anonymity.
Crip, it is said, left the road and became a justice of the peace
in Indiana. But Pop never broke the tentacles of wanderlust.
Hoboes after the turn of the century told of seeing the aged
wanderer on a branch line in Pennsylvania, still nabbing an
occasional slow freight.

The road offered startling contrasts. A writer for the *Atlantic Monthly* in 1907 stumbled across one Jack the Hobo
lounging on a grassy field, sunning himself and his just-
washed shirt. The hobo enraptured his audience with a peroration on the glories of vagabond existence: "I wist you'd
seen the rivers I seen. I seen places where you wouldn't

never want to do nothin' all day, but just lay there, smellin'
them flowers and listin' to them birds. I came out here to
wash my shirt. I start out to work Monday, takin' a job to
cut grass. Maybe I work all day Monday; maybe I don't.
Some weeks I stick it out till Tuesday, or even till Thursday
or Friday, but I get to feelin' uneasy. 'Hell!' I say to myself.
'I just got to wash my shirt.' . . . Then I come out here and
build me a camp fire, and cook something to eat and lay
claim on my back, and just enjoy till I think that shirt of
mine is dry." Jack might think the shirt still wet a week later.
This was hobo Nirvana where the pie was not in the sky but
in a life of repose and leisure on the green earth. This was
one face of hobo life. In the same year that Jack and his shirt
found their way into print, the annual report of the Interstate Commerce Commission announced that nearly 25,000
railroad trespassers had been killed from 1901 to 1905.
Slightly more than that had been injured and maimed. Many
railroads maintained private "tramp graveyards" in which
they buried the nameless dead without inquest. This was
another face of hobo life.

You could meet all kinds of guys on the road. One 'bo in
the early years remembered freighting it in Michigan with
about thirty others during a time when railroad dicks were
making wholesale arrests throughout the state. When the
subject of possible legal recourse came up, one tough-look-
ing stiff suddenly launched into a learned disquisition on vagrancy laws in several states. Buttressing his arguments with
case citations by the score, the guy left thirty mouths agape.
He afterward confessed to having a law degree.

Hobo Bill, a gregarious veteran who hit the road in 1919,
is another of the 'boes who make the yearly trek to Britt. Although advancing years have curtailed his freight-jumping
activities, he still gets around the country in a camper. He
remembers jungling with another 'bo who hit the road

strictly as a matter of choice. Long after leaving the vagabond life for another career, the friend, Bill says, kept in
touch until his death. The friend was Winthrop Rockefeller.
From Jack London to William O. Douglas, the road has carried many men who later became prominent. Clark Gable,
before his Rhett Butler days, tramped across the country.
On one of his sojourns, a young, rather emaciated Gable
landed in Butte, Montana, with no money or friends. A hobo
from Texas named Jack Bates came to the rescue with a huge
meal and a five-spot. The two rode the freights to Portland,
where they went separate ways. Gable often spoke of Jack
Bates. In an interview in 1939 the screen star said that the
hobo had saved his life.

But most of those in the road army were anonymous stiffs,
a desperate throng of individuals wandering the country for
numberless reasons, alienated from traditional American
life-styles, homeless with few or no ties to family or community. It was in the hobo jungles that they found a fleeting
sense of social bond. Usually located just outside of town,
near running water and the tracks, the jungle served as pub,
restaurant, hotel, literary gathering place, and information
center. Old discarded tin cans became cooking utensils;
branches became clotheslines. Each new traveler passing
through contributed wood for the fire and food for the pot, if
he could. Here the 'boes could swap yarns, share the mulligan, and take on traveling partners. The jungle was probably
given its name, Frisco Jack says, because of the weeds and
underbrush normally surrounding it.

The characters that passed through a jungle had many different backgrounds. Ben Reitman, hobo, radical, political
gadfly, lover of anarchist Emma Goldman, and student of
social outcasts, remembered the first hobo jungle he saw at
the turn of the century as a young boy tramp or punk.
There was Cleveland Mushy, an itinerant umbrella mender

who had traveled through Nebraska and Wyoming before the Civil War. Mushy, with his prominent Tolstoyesque whiskers, looked like a character out of Maxim Gorky's "A Night's Lodging." There was Denver Red, a tall, popular stiff wracked with consumption who used his affliction most effectively as a con. Red said that his tuberculosis was a lucky break, a good graft. It gave him a legitimate excuse and much sympathy for "throwing the feet." There was also Irish, a vigorous worker, fighter, drinker, and womanizer, who could, drunk or sober, talk and sing up a storm about his native land. New Orleans Slim traveled with his son Louisiana Blue. Slim, a malarial, crusty Johnny Reb, hated Yankees and blamed the blacks for the country's and his own problems. He had tramped all the southern states without doing time on a chain gang or charity farm, a rare feat in that part of the country but not too surprising given his background and attitudes. There was Sailor Bill, an anchor tattooed on his chest, a bottle of rum in his pocket, an endless stream of seafaring exaggeration in his repertoire. There was Blackie, an ex-lineman for a telegraph company who was on the run from the family of a pregnant girl. And there was Rags, a massive, hairy, lousy gentleman dressed in an assortment of clothes including four coats, three pairs of pants, and three shirts. In each pocket was something— books, food, needles and thread, old pieces of iron, scraps of paper. His outside coat was covered with approximately fifty different badges and buttons. Rags was a walking trash can.

The talk in the jungles was of the road and work, the hostile towns and railroad dicks, the trains and the narrow escapes. The jungle campfire was the forum for the hobo Homers to spin their various tales. Many of the stories were grounded in fact but embellished beyond recognition. Not surprisingly, hobo audiences were treated to a number of

yarns which had suspiciously similar plots. One of the favor-
ites told again and again with minor twists and personal
touches was a simple one: hobo drops from a boxcar, knocks
at the back door of a mansion, is invited in by the attractive
lady of the house. It is the servants' day off, naturally. After
the 'bo offers his tale of need, the lady invites him to sit
down to one of the finest meals he's ever tasted. It turns out
that the husband is a railroad official with a closet full of un-
used $100 suits. The lady, smitten with more than sympathy
for the handsome vagabond, offers him a shower, a new suit,
a five-dollar bill, and herself for the afternoon. Late in the
day the lady warns, "Don't ever come around here again.
My husband would shoot you." Our roving hero gallantly
bids adieu and hops on an outbound freight to new romance
and adventure.

Jungle behavior was limited by a code of ethics and enforced by ad hoc groups. Crimes such as jackrolling, wasting
food, destroying equipment, and leaving dirty utensils were
all punished by expulsion, forced labor, and head busting.
Contrary to legend, most hoboes regarded dirt as a distasteful occupational hazard and took great pains to conquer it.
At the end of a ride on the freights, the hobo usually had the
evidence all over him. Grimy from billows of smoke and
soot, covered with brick dust, coal dust, or anything else on
the floors of boxcars, the newly arrived passenger was not
only an easy mark for local police but extremely uncomfort-
able. Bathing and "boiling up" in the jungle were rituals to
which the men gave great care. Many 'boes used pieces of
broken bottles to shave. They scrubbed discarded cooking
utensils with sand and water.

Jungle nights could reverberate with song and poetry and
jokes. They could also, on occasion, offer Bacchanalian
feasts. One world-traveled 'bo, looking back on some of
those meals with longing, wrote in the thirties, "I have

wined and dined in many places, in great banquet halls with scientists and statesmen at my side, lunched in the boulevards of Paris with a beautiful woman, in faraway Persia eaten in a tent with those whose language I could not understand and I have also eaten a last meal with a condemned man who was to take the rope to the Great Beyond in the morning. But I do not believe that any of those meals satisfied my stomach, stimulated my brain and gave me a better sense of fellowship than the meals I have eaten in the jungles with my hobo friends."

The freights, the succession of jobs, and the jungle sanctuaries made up the hobo's life for most of the year. But in the winter the fight for survival was even more challenging. Their peripatetic wanderings of summer over, most 'boes, like bees returning to the hives, headed to the cities.

Wednesday, February 18, 1914, 11:30 P.M., the Marshall Hotel, San Francisco. The building is used by city authorities for housing the unemployed. With heavy rain pounding outside, 132 men huddle in one room side by side in rows on the floor. As others, soaking wet, stand around a single stove trying to dry their clothes, an eerie steam rises. The air is foul. In the next room 187 men sleep fitfully on newspaper bedding and shoe pillows. Next door 211 bodies pack the windowsills as well as the floor. On stairway landings, in the halls, against the doors, men battle the odor, the rats, the bugs, and each other. In the upper rooms hundreds more squeeze together, a total of more than 1,200 in the hotel with others trying to get in. A man in the last stages of consumption coughs and spits. Another, who had been living in a tent a few blocks away and had sought cover from the cold rain, decides to return to his tent.

To West Madison Street in Chicago, the nation's preeminent main stem, the 'boes came in the winters. Also to the Bowery in New York, Pratt Street in Baltimore, South Main

Street in Los Angeles, Third Street in San Francisco. In the city the wintering hobo became one in a sea of aimless, lost souls. The skid roads were all of a familiar character: gospel missions, cheap rooming houses and hotels, secondhand clothes stores, barber colleges, greasy spoons, soup lines, checkrooms for baggage, pawnshops, liquor stores, whorehouses, and a ripe choice of bars. In the Municipal Lodging House in New York, the Wayfarers' Lodge in Philadelphia, the Hawkins Street Woodyard in Boston, the City Lodging House in Washington, D.C., in jails, almshouses, calabooses, missions, flophouses, water closets, livery stables, in alley doors, hoboes looked for shelter. Some were even driven to the steam gratings which, as a last resort, could keep a man from freezing. Civic organizations catered to the migrants' needs with municipal hotels and woodyards; ecclesiastical charities such as the Salvation Army and the Volunteers of America offered some relief; and local rescue missions did what they could with meager finances and poor facilities.

The Rescue Mission in Colorado Springs in the thirties took its revival and evangelical duties very seriously, as did most missions. One 'bo told a writer several decades ago about straggling in before seven o'clock one night, his angry stomach in rebellion. The mission leader, a young woman, began to lead the men in hymns. At nine o'clock they were still singing. "We expected any moment to be invited to eat," the hobo recalled, "but it takes time to purify the soul. 'Has anyone a testimony to make?' asked the leader. No one budged. 'Who will testify that he has seen the light?' she continued. 'Who will seek forgiveness for his sins?' The man on my left stood up to testify. He said he had been a gambler, a drinker, a smoker, the worst of sinners, but the Lord had saved him. I am inclined to think that his testimony was the sudden offspring of hunger. 'Glory be to God,' said the pleased leader. 'Hallelujah, praise the Lord,' chimed in her cohorts. The leader and her friends got down on their knees to testify. They screamed, shouted to God, and wept audibly. Each one seemed bent on drowning the voices of the other." At nine-thirty, the mission leaders, to the relief of the men, stopped their shouting and ranting. The food was apparently on the way. But wait! The leader announced that Mother W. would begin the sermon. "The man on my left who had given testimony whispered, 'Let's get the hell out of this madhouse. It'll be morning before we eat.' I agreed."

One of the best-known hobo songs, "The Preacher and the Slave," perhaps said it best:

> *Long-haired preachers come out every night,*
> *Try to tell you what's wrong and what's right;*
> *But when asked about something to eat,*
> *They will answer in voices so sweet:*
>> *You will eat, bye and bye,*
>> *In that glorious land in the sky;*
>> *Work and pray, live on hay*
>> *You'll get pie in the sky when you die.*

But not all sky pilots were despised by the hobo community. Three hundred ragged men knelt on the floor of a dingy mission in Chicago in 1912 to pray for Dan Martin, ex-hobo turned evangelist. Martin, who died later in the evening, was regarded by the fraternity as Chicago's greatest mission director. He had worked himself to exhaustion trying to save them from the barrelhouses and gutters he had known so well personally in earlier years. One of his closest friends said that Dan Martin had saved 2,000 to 3,000 souls a year. "And they stay saved."

In the cities, hoboes had more to fight than the cold and hunger. The 'boes could quickly lose a winter's stake to the saloons, the whores, and the gamblers. They were often rolled by other drifters and thieves. Most 'boes slept on their shoes and hid any cash, but when drunk they were easy marks. Eyeglasses, glass eyes, false teeth, army discharges, photographs—anything and everything could disappear. A hobo who had been rolled in a lodging house complained, "Somebody robbed me of a new pair of socks. I paid a dime for them, and last night was the first time I took 'em off in two weeks."

The employment sharks were also waiting on the main stem. Sometimes employed directly by the farmers or lumber barons or, more often, working hand in glove with them, the sharks charged the unemployed men fees for locating jobs. After the shark pocketed the fee and sent the stiff on his way, the boss would give him a job for a few days, fire him, and receive a kickback from the shark. A perpetual stream of workers going to and leaving jobs made for lucrative collusion.

As the floater wandered along rows of employment agencies on the stem, posters beckoned describing precious jobs that paid good wages and called for short hours. "Go to the Dakotas." "Work the harvests in an idyllic farm setting." "Make a fantastic stake." What the hobo found in the hop fields and timberlands was less than Valhalla—hovels and shacks, poor water, a wage scale that barely allowed the worker to break even. At one hop ranch in California the owners provided six toilets for 2,300 workers.

The intolerable labor conditions, the stringent vagrancy laws, the harassment by law enforcement officials, the misery of cities, all further alienated the American hobo from the rest of society. But in the early part of the century, the workers of the road found new outlets for their discontent. One was in the Industrial Workers of the World. The radical Wobblies represented to the average 'bo those things he could see in his own life—disaffiliation, disaffection, unrest, rebellion. So great became the power of the IWW among the hoboes of the West by 1915 that the red membership card became the unofficial passport for riding the rails.

Other organizations and unions, founded especially for
the improvement of the lot of the migratory worker, appeared. Hoboes and their benefactors set up Hobo Colleges
where instructors taught survival techniques, philosophy,
law, literature, and other courses. They began to hold conventions such as the one in Britt. They started to publish
newspapers. Some wrote articles and published books.
Through all of this activity, the 'boes began to share more
fully a sense of fraternity with their brothers. From jungle
campfires, from boxcars and jail cells, from Wobbly rallies,
came songs, poems, stories, and lore, all manifestations of a
remarkable subculture. They wrote and sang of railroads, of
solitude and pain, of working and doing time, of the grandeur of the country, of the power of the railroads, of the vir-
tues of freedom and the open road, of the injustices to working stiffs of the country. From "Where Is My Wandering
Boy Tonight?" to "Wabash Cannonball" to "Meet Me in the
Jungles, Louie" the hobo began to leave his mark on American folk heritage. When he waxed philosophical, a hobo
might even trace his lineage to another model of nonconfor-
mity, Jesus Christ, or, as he was dubbed by some 'boes,
Jerusalem Slim. In 1921 an IWW publication carried a poem
in which Jesus admonishes a scissorbill, a worker with no
class consciousness:

> *You scoff at the rebel and lynch him till dead*
> *But I was an outcast and they called me a Red,*
> *You call me Christ Jesus with intelligence dim*
> *But I was a rebel called Jerusalem Slim.*
> *And my brother: the outcast, the rebel and the tramp*
> *And not the religious, the scab or the scamp . . .*

As increasing mechanization brought shorter harvest periods, as the advent of the automobile made it possible for the
unemployed nonhobo to reach work sites quickly, many

western industries by the end of the twenties took on a new character. The floaters and blackbirds were not as indispensable and not as much in evidence as they once had been. Also, the modern technology of the railroads, with their high-powered diesel engines and computerized, automatically regulated systems, had a dramatic impact on the hobo community. "You can't hook a train on the go anymore," says Sparky Smith, another aging rail rider at the Britt convention. "You have to nab them in the yards." Sparky's graybeard appearance and the friendships he has cultivated in years on the tracks do land him occasional free rides in the cabooses or engines. But for Sparky and the rest of his compatriots the life is not the same. Not only have the railroad systems been mechanized in recent years, the number of lines has been drastically reduced. The railroad had been the matrix of the hobo experience and, with its demise, the lifeblood of hoboism was drained. Hood River Blackie, a longtime 'bo who has for several decades collected hobo biographies, declared a few years ago, "Someday very soon the passing of the hobo will be complete, and he will go the way of the buffalo hunter and the mountain man. No more will his ear bound at the whistle of a steam locomotive, for it too has passed into history. No more will we see his lonely campfire somewhere along the tracks out of Omaha or Cheyenne. No more will he see the starlight on the rails or hear the thunder of the fast express. He will sleep in fields where roses fade, under the moss and ferns."

Some of the old 'boes refuse to give up. Chicken Red Donovan ran away from home in 1898 on an outbound freight. Eighty years later he did it again, this time from a nursing home. When you're hooked, you're hooked. Propping a plank against the welcome side of a vacant boxcar, the ancient Red managed to crawl up and steal a ride. When discovered at a town down the line, Red was asked whether he wasn't too old for this sort of thing. The annoyed old 'bo retorted, "Not this hobo. I have been riding since 1898, by damn!"

To a few—to Steam Train Maury, the Pennsylvania Kid, Hood River Blackie, and the others—the road is still a challenge, still represents freedom and defiance. But the long rides on the top deck, the harrowing chases with railroad dicks, the wandering from state to state and job to job, the excitement and victories—all of this, with the loneliness and fear, fades into memory. As Virginia Slim, a hobo troubadour from Richmond, put it:

> *And few are left who know their rhyme*
> *Since long ago when they departed*
> *Over run by changing time*
> *So pay attention now my children*
> *And the old story I will tell*
> *About the jungles and the freight trains*
> *About a breed of men who fell.*

2/ On the Road

TRAIN FLIPPIN'

> Listen to the jingle, the rumble and the roar,
> As she glides along the woodlands, through hills and by the
>   shore,
> Hear the mighty rush of the engine, hear those lonesome
>   hoboes squall,
> While traveling through the jungle on the Wabash
>   Cannonball.

THIS WAS the hobo phantom train. If sailors had their spectral ship, *The Flying Dutchman*, the hoboes had their Wabash Cannonball. From Minnesota to Memphis to Mattoon, flying through Colorado, highballing from California to Labrador, the Cannonball made its mythical run, toting its passengers to visionary Elysian fields. Like the lemonade springs and the lakes of stew and whiskey of the legendary Big Rock Candy Mountains, the hobo fantasy paradise, the image of the hobo glory train was a stark contrast to the 'boes' real world on the tracks.

In May 1869 the Union Pacific announced the grand opening of the Atlantic to Pacific railroad. Through to San Francisco in less than four days, the announcements proclaimed, and no dangers from the sea. Passengers were urged to travel for pleasure or health or business through the invigorating air of the Rockies; lounge in luxury; dine in elegance; sleep in the Pullman "palaces"; seek their fortune in gold and silver in Nevada, Arizona, Oregon, Idaho, and California; stake a claim to wealth and romance. This was the beginning of the golden age of the railroad. To the rhythmic beat of the gandy-dancer sledge, a giant network of track spun westward. In 1850 the railroad system could boast only

9,000 miles of track; twenty years later more than 70,000 miles would cross the country. The railroad became the great tool of industrial expansion as it shuttled crops and minerals from distant farms and mines and carried the products to newly opened markets. It shuttled people, too—speculators, small businessmen, farmers, hundreds of thousands drawn by the alluring vision of the West.

As the advertisements promised, a well-heeled traveler could ride in opulent accommodations—plush chairs that converted into sleeping berths, ornate furnishings, dainty linen, shiny brass spittoons. In the Silver Palace Hotel Car a traveler, surrounded by Victorian brocaded furniture, fine crystal, stained-glass windows, and Brussels carpets, could feast on ham and tongue, blue-winged teal and other delicacies, served by a staff of starched-collar waiters. As the western sky framed the majestic locomotive against a mountain backdrop, the traveler probably heard the beat of the wheels as the beat of America's future, a glorious harbinger of progress.

But hold on! What was that dark form under the car, inches from the cinders, swaying precariously with the curves? that other murky shape lying on top of one of the cars, spreadeagled, hanging on? And there was another—grimy, soot covered, like a chimney sweep fresh from his labors! A hobo writer once observed, "Inside the passengers sat, warm and soft on the upholstered seats, or lay sleeping in their berths. And on the prow of the giant land-ship stood three muffled figures, shivering but dauntless, carried on—through bitter cold and smoke and turmoil, danger of arrest or of beating—towards the harvest jobs that would earn them sustenance for a short space." Was this another harbinger?

Henry George wrote in 1879, "The 'tramp' comes with the locomotive, and almshouses and prisons are as surely the marks of 'material progress' as are costly dwellings, rich warehouses, and magnificent churches." If the locomotive had created the traveler in the Silver Palace Hotel Car, if it had produced the Harrimans, the Goulds, and the Fiskes, it had also brought Philadelphia Shorty and Providence Bob.

"A flight of alien, unclean birds" descending on the Midwest harvest fields, Hamlin Garland called the roving homeless in *A Son of the Middle Border*. The image mocked Herman Melville's smug observation in 1849 that "such a being as a beggar is almost unknown; and to be a born American citizen seems a guarantee against pauperism." In 1873, depression had struck. A European financial crisis had seriously affected the United States economy as foreign businessmen withdrew American investments. Jay Cooke and Company, the powerful banking house and financial agent for the Northern Pacific Railway, failed. The American financial structure, weakened by wild speculation in railroads and overexpansion in almost every part of the economy, began to crumble. More than 100 financial houses collapsed, business and insurance companies closed, and railroad construction, the nation's booming industry, boomed no longer. Nearly half a million railroad workers lost their jobs. Unemployment hit the foundries, the rolling mills, and the machine shops. Some estimates set the jobless figure at 40 percent nationwide. Bread and soup lines queued up in small towns as well as in the major metropolitan areas. In Dedham, Massachusetts, the town's selectmen complained that the feeding and sheltering of hungry, homeless men had drained available resources. Nearly 3,000 wanderers asked for relief in one year. Similar reports appeared from police departments, almshouses, state farms, and correction houses across the land. In 1874, Philadelphia lodged over 60,000 transients, more than the population of its most densely populated ward.

Walking Toward L.A., March, 1937

*Providence Bob and Philadelphia Shorty
on their 'tickets', 1894*

A 'BO, Yakima Valley, Washington, August, 1939

Jungle, Downer's Grove, Illinois, 1924

Jungling, 1895

(above)
*A Night's Lodging,
Chicago, 1913*

O— Turn Right

—O   "   Le

Ò   straight ahead

ɪɪɪɪɪɪɪ { a comb has teeth —
            so has a dog

Ⱶ   Top Hat

8 ∆∆∆ — Kind woman

∧ — Run Like H—

*Hobo Signs as Drawn by
The Cheyenne Kid
at Britt Convention, 1978*

If the depression had driven many of the unemployed to the road, others had been there since the war. A Massachusetts police official, lamenting the growing number of vagabonds he had recently confronted in his state, wrote, "The bummers of our armies could not give up their habits of roving and marauding, and settle down to the honest and industrious duties of the citizen . . . but preferred a life of vagrancy." Unsettled war veterans, workers displaced and uprooted by economic pressures, young boys with families wrenched apart by the horrors of depression—thousands began to drift. And most turned to the railroad. Many of the burgeoning force of nomads had grown up in the towns along the tracks, and the sounds, smells, and language of the railroad had been with them from an early age. Many had walked the tracks to school; some had flipped slow-moving freights before they could read their primers. For many, the freight yards and cinder beds were playgrounds. The short hops of one or two miles in a side-door Pullman became ten- or twenty- or fifty-mile treks to more distant towns. The boy who rode 100 miles one day likely dreamed of riding 1,-000 the next.

Roving Bill Aspinwall was one who logged many miles. A former correspondent for a rural newspaper, Aspinwall had been wounded in the Civil War and had later taken to the bottle and the road. Earning enough money to get by as a mushfaker, or umbrella mender, Bill slept most nights in the boxcars or, on cold nights, warmed himself in secluded woods with fires made out of railroad ties. When he learned that a Hartford sociologist named John J. McCook was undertaking a study of tramps and hoboes, Aspinwall began a correspondence with McCook that lasted nearly a quarter of a century. From inside boxcars and along the tracks, Bill jotted numerous letters to McCook describing his life on the road and his encounters on the trains.

I have walked about 4 miles from where I started last night and there came up a Heavy Rain   I made for a Barn along side of the road and am now safely domiciled in the Barn on some Hay. Have eat nothing to-day and my stomach begins to feel a little Weak   I will give you a little of my experience. About four years ago I was in Joplin Missouri near Indian Ter. I wanted to go to Pleasant Hill, Mo about one hundred miles north. Joplin is the end of a Division of the South West Branch of the Mo Pacific R.R. There was a Passenger Train left Joplin for Pleasant Hill about 3 o'clock in the morning. I went down in the yard where the Cars were that was going on that Train   A RR man gave me the information   I got on top of one of the coaches about half hour before the Train left and got near a stove Pipe so as I could Hold on by this time the Engine came out and coupled on and away she went   I thought I never saw a Train go faster. The Roof of the Coach was Rounding or oval and you can bet I Hung on to that stove pipe with a vengence. My Hair would raise on my Head some times as I would come near Rolling of but I hung on to it until I got to a station within about ten miles of Pleasant Hill. Then it was day light and every one could see me from the station Platform and they began to laugh and make remarks The conductor got on to me and climbed upon Break wheel and asked me what I was doing up there   I told Him Riding of Course. He said come down and I came down and the People and Passengers Began to laugh and ask me questions   I was one of the Dirtiest smoked up mortals you ever saw. I would of Passed for a Colerd man   I did not Blame the People for laughing   The train started and the People on Platform yelled catch Her   I did so and Rode five miles farther on Her and she stoped again   I got of and walked into Pleasant Hill   I hung around there until night and there was a fast express Bound for St. Louis on Main line Mo. Pac. RR   I jumped the Blind Baggage of Her in Rear of Engine and when we got under good Headway the Engineer and Fireman saw me and took the Hose and Began throwing water on me. I had to take it as I could not get of the train going at the rate of 60 miles an Hour. I was soaking wet and it was tolerable cold and I was shivering. I got of the first stop and went and got on the next car in Rear where they could not get at me with their water and went with the train into St. Louis.

The railroad and its siren song, offering opportunity, adventure, and escape, lured thousands to the road. Walt Whitman paid homage to the spell of its enchanting, awesome steam beasts:

> *Thy black cylindric body, golden brass and silvery steel,*
> *Thy ponderous side-bars, parallel and connecting rods,*
> *gyrating, shuttling at thy sides,*
> *Thy metrical, now swelling pant and roar, now tapering in*
> *the distance,*
> *Thy great protruding head-light fix'd in front,*
> *Thy long, pale, floating vapor-pennants, tinged with deli-*
> *cate purple,*
> *Thy dense and murky clouds out-belching from thy smoke-*
> *stack,*
> *Thy knitted frame, thy springs and valves, the tremulous*
> *twinkle of thy wheels,*
> *Thy train of cars behind, obedient, merrily following, . . .*

If Whitman felt exhilaration at the sight of a passing train, the growing horde of road wanderers knew another kind of exhilaration. For fledgling knights of the road the train became a rite of passage. To deck a rattler, to hold down a fast express, to ride the brake beams with death only inches away in the cinders and the gleaming, knife-edged wheels, was a badge of initiation into the fraternity.

Veteran riders were students of train anatomy. They could recite the cubic **footage** of various cars, their vintage and makers, could carefully explain how they operated and for what purposes, could point out the crevices and crannies which, with a degree of ingenuity, were transformed into riding places. Lack of such detailed knowledge could lead to

sudden disaster. One conductor recalled a jumper who made
the fatal mistake of riding on the brake beam of an engine
tank. When the engineers routinely released steam and
scalding water under the cab, a procedure known as "blowing out the engine," the surreptitious rider received the full
force and was, as the conductor put it, "blown into eter-
nity."

The old-timers will tell you that freight hopping was not
for the dullard but for the ingenious, keen-witted, and swift
afoot. Only the elite rarely bit the ballast. From softsoaping
the brakemen to holding down the fast freights in storms
and bitter cold to dodging the bulls, the train jumper faced
formidable challenges. Intense, workmanlike, he knew full
well the consequences of one misgauged leap. In the art of
corralling a ride without being spotted by bulls and shacks,
the trick was always to keep in front of the train—lie low
ahead of the target as it left the station; nab it as it passed;
find a place to ride out the distance between stops; jump off
on the opposite side of the station just before the train
stopped; run ahead and find another hiding place before it
started up again; repeat the process. Tom Kromer in *Waiting for Nothing* told how it felt flipping a hot, fast freight: "I
judge my distance. I start running along this track. I hold my
hand up to the side of these cars. They brush my fingers as
they fly by. I feel this step hit my fingers and dive. My fingers get hold of it. I grab it as tight as I can. I think my arms
will be jerked out of their sockets. My ribs feel like they are
smashed. I hang on. I made it."

Alan Pinkerton, founder of the Pinkerton National Detective Agency, the skillfully trained, fearfully effective army-
for-hire paid by industrialists to break the heads of unionist
strikers and other enemies of the capitalist system, published
in 1878 a work entitled *Strikers, Communists, Tramps and
Detectives*. Pinkerton, whose organization would later,

under the employ of the railroads, break tramp heads, described one of the early train jumpers: "A tramp boarded the train at Cheyenne, climbed to the top of the coach and enjoyed hugely his elegant and rapid manner of making his journey until Sherman was reached. At that point the engineer got a glimpse of him and he at once began throwing a heavy shower of cinders and increased the speed to the utmost power of the engine . . . the cinders burned into his clothes, cut his arms and legs and face." When the rider later descended from his nest, Pinkerton remarked, the boy of nineteen looked more like a man of sixty.

The train jumper had several choices once he boarded. The "blind baggage," the front platform of the baggage car of passenger trains, was a convenient and popular, if somewhat vulnerable, perch. The door leading to the platform was not used because of the baggage inside piled against it. The blind thus provided a relatively cozy, commodious nook. If the jumper were detected, however, he was, like the jumper in Alan Pinkerton's account, an easy target for water hoses or showers of coal or hot ash from the more sadistic firemen. This was the great uncertainty, the disposition of the fireman—was he "A-1" or "horstile"? Riding the blind, one hobo thought, was like riding the "nose of a great steel projectile hurtling like a comet through flying stardust and frightened planets." The dust most riders of the rattlers tasted, however, was not from the stars but from smokestack and tender. And although the blind was one of the less hazardous riding spaces, tragedy was only a false step away. William Davies, English tramp writer and poet, lost part of a leg attempting to leap on a blind with another jumper. After the comrade had successfully mounted the blind platform, he thoughtlessly left little room for Davies, who desperately embraced a handlebar on the ever-faster-racing train. "I shouted to him to clear the step," Davies painfully recalled.

"This he proceeded to do, very deliberately, I thought, for the train was now going at a very rapid rate. My foot came short of the step, and I fell, and, still clinging to the handle-bar, was dragged several yards before I relinquished my hold. And there I lay for several minutes, feeling a little shaken, whilst the train passed swiftly on into the darkness." Until he glanced at the blood-splattered ground, Davies didn't realize the extent of his injury. The razor wheels had severed his right foot just above the ankle.

A teenage Jack London gloried in his rail conquests, reveling in playing the tantalizing mouse in chases with stalking train cats: "The train pulls out. There is a lantern on the first blind. I lie low, and see the peering shack go by. But there is also a lantern on the second blind. That shack spots me and calls to the shack who has gone past on the first blind. Both jump off. Never mind. I'll take the third blind and deck her. But heavens, there is a lantern on the third blind, too. It is the conductor. I let it go by. At any rate I have now the full train-crew in front of me. I turn and run back in the opposite direction to what the train is going. I look over my shoulder. All three lanterns are on the ground and wobbling along in pursuit. I sprint. Half the train has gone by, and it is going quite fast, when I spring aboard. I know that the two shacks and the conductor will arrive like ravening wolves in about two seconds. I spring upon the wheel of the handbrake, get my hands on the curved ends of the roofs, and muscle my-self up to the decks; while my disappointed pursuers . . . howl curses up at me and say unsocial things about my an-cestors."

The jumpers rode in boxcars, on gondolas, in reefers, or on the top decks. A brakeman once discovered a freight jumper in a boxcar load of mules astride one of the beasts. When asked what he was doing, the rider laconically mut-tered, "Driving mules to Chattanooga."

Some rode in battery boxes that hung beneath passenger coaches. Armed with wire to keep the door shut, a resourceful stiff might pretzel himself inside and ride unmolested for hundreds of miles. A hobo named Frisco told of a battery-box trip from Chicago to California:

Some trip that was. I'll never forget it. I had a lot o' trouble gettin' in the box without somebody seein' me, and I went down to the yards hours before the train pulled out, too. I had a bunch of sandwiches on me, and a bottle of water with a little sugar in it. I just laid quiet till the train clicked out of "Chi." Three days I was in there. The grub and the water lasted me two days, so I had to go hungry the rest of the time. I didn't mind that so much, but the cramps in my back tortured me till I nearly went bughouse. You know, you're doubled up like a jacknife and ain't got room to stretch. . . . I had a deck of cards with me, and once I tried to play solitaire; but the dust was too thick, and the dark strained my eyes. Nothin' to do but sleep and think. I had no idea of time or where I was. I knew when it was daylight and when it was dark; that's all. After I had been there a week, it seemed, it got infernal cold in the night, and I figured I was crossing the mountains somewhere in Arizona or New Mexico. I shivered till I thought I'd shake myself to pieces. Then suddenly . . . the damned screw-eye flew out, with my wire wrapped in it. The door flopped open, and the wind came at me ice-cold and yelpin' like a pack o' dogs. The limited was hittin' her up fifty mile an hour, anyway. The door slammed up and down, and I thought every second she'd strike a high tie, and rip the ol' battery box, with me in, right out from under the car and send us a-smashin' to hell. Holy smokes! I was scairt. Then the train hit a curve so fast I had to fight like a whitehead to keep her from pitchin' me out. I was paddlin' and clawin' with both hands and feet like a mouse on a treadwheel. She straightened purty soon, and I was all right. Then I pokes my head out a little ways, and the wind almost blinded me while I was grabbin' for that jumpin' wire. Before I knew it though, zowy! the door flew up and caught me right on the bean.

Knocked me silly. By and by the door flew shut with an awful wham. I was in a daze but I managed to get my hooks on that wire before she flew open again. And I swung on to her most of the night just like a guy that's tryin' to hold a bull calf that's rippin' and r'arin' and lungin'. My head ached fierce, and a bump crowned the top of her the size of half a grape-fruit. When the train slowed down at a town I got the screw back in place, but I was so nervous I couldn't sleep all the rest of the trip.

The veteran blowed-in-the-glass stiff was most often well prepared for battle. He might be decked out in rubbers to protect his feet from abrasion and to make his movements more catlike; goggles to shield his eyes from the biting winds and smoke; and gloves to protect his hands from blistering. One conductor told of one such fully equipped young jumper on a cowcatcher. With a heavily padded hat, three or four layers of sweaters, a pair of football trousers, and his lower legs in thick stockings, the rider was virtually a cocoon, ready to absorb the shocks of a sixty-mile-an-hour limited. On the cowcatcher you needed all the help you could get. One 'bo recounted the joys of his first and only journey in such a fashion: "There was yours truly smilin' like a basket o' chips on the cowcatcher. But I didn't smile long. That engine was a passenger engine and kicked up an awful wind. Open yer mouth, and she'd blow you wrong side out, and so cold she felt like an icicle laid against your eyeballs. . . . Well, as I set there slappin' myself tryin' to keep warm, the headlight sprayed out across the prairie and attracted all the bugs in Kansas. My mouth and eyes and shirt got full of 'em, and them big, shiny, black bugs hurt, too, when they hit you between the eyes." Ahead, the 'bo glimpsed an old white cow contentedly munching her cud. The wailing rush of the train brought little more than a blink from the cow but stark terror from the train jumper wedged up front. "I sort o' slid down on the back of my neck and h'isted my heels up in the air so's bossy would hit them first. Well, just before we reached her, she ambled calmly off the track, flickin' her tail. . . . Don't never mention cowcatcher to me again. It makes me nervous to talk about it."

If riding the cowcatcher was a harrowing business, the underbellies of the trains held out the ultimate challenge— riding the rods. The target for the jumper was a single rod which crossed under the four-wheel truck of the passenger car. About four feet long, the rod stretched laterally between the cross-partition of the truck and the axle. The method of mounting was complex to say the least. The jumper seized one of the gunnels, iron braces that formed supporting trusses underneath the cars, put his foot to rest on a brake beam, hung by his arms, his back to the rail, and contorted himself to a doubled-up standing position outside the truck. He then squeezed into the space between the tip of the truck and the bottom of the car and wormed along over the revolving axle to the cross rod. Squirming down onto the rod with his back to the truck, one shoulder to the cross-partition and another one within inches of a wheel that could instantly become a cleaver, he took out his "ticket," a thick board about a foot and a half long with a groove hewed midway along its length to allow it to slip onto the rod. Perched on his board, the rider was free from view if not from peril. Barring attacks by bulls, some of whom were not above dangling long deadly pieces of iron onto the tracks to ricochet around the vulnerable rider, and barring the onset of sleep or fatal slips of the ticket, the rider was assured of a ride at least to the next division stop, a rollicking ride with the wheel buzzing at his arm, his body swaying and jolting with the movements of massive car above, his face pitted by splattering gravel. The men who dared this mode of travel and survived could justly lay claim to train-jumping knighthood.

If the train itself didn't get you, train crews and railroad agents might. And some were brutal. A few didn't hesitate to use train jumpers as rifle targets. To the bull kings, the freight was the royal domain; interlopers and violaters were spared little mercy. The name of Denver Bob of Amarillo became in the hobo world a despised legend, as did that of Jeff Carr of Cheyenne. Jeff Carr—the very name sent shudders through jungles far and wide—the terror of the West, the cinder dick whose sole mission in life seemed to be to exterminate the hobo and tramp infestation. Old Jeff played the part to the hilt—long, menacing black mustache curling around his mouth, guns strapped to his sides. One young road novice was awed: "Well, boy, we rode a blind out o' Cheyenne . . . dey was t'ree ginks on it wid us; and purty soon a guy comes ridin' up side o' de train like hell splittin' . . . he reaches for one o' de ginks and yanks him off'n de blind, and den ketches annuder one by de belt and trows 'im across de horse's neck an' starts shootin'." Many stiffs made a special effort to avoid Cheyenne.

One 'bo wrote in a hobo newspaper in 1919 of being pulled off a freight by six railroad dicks at Elkton, Maryland, a town along the line of the Valley Railroad, the "Punk and Plaster" route. One fellow passenger who refused to give his age when questioned was beaten to a pulp with billies and blackjacks. The dicks got fifty cents a head from their company for capturing drifters and this night's catch was a good one. A black jumper who had decked one of the cars leaped from the top to a ditch about nine feet below ground level and became a target for one of the gat-toting bounty hunters. As the dick blazed away, another was shouting, "Don't try to catch the son of a bitch. Shoot him dead." And he did.

The bulls found special delight in throwing off black jumpers. One 'bo remembered being caught on a train in Arkansas in the twenties with several blacks. The white trainmen, brandishing clubs, methodically marched along from car to car viciously throwing off only the blacks. The white stiffs were allowed to stay on if they had four bits. But in some areas of the country there were other train jumpers who stood even lower in the caste lines than the blacks. In Arizona and other southwestern states, hobos told of Mexicans being ditched in the most isolated areas of the desert to face probable death. "We were far out in the desert when our freight stopped," a hobo recalled. "It had quite a load of hoboes, most white, but also a few blacks and more Mexicans." Three dicks with clubs and flashlights began searching the train. "Any greasers here?" one snapped. As all the hoboes began to leave the train, the dicks told the whites and blacks to stay on. When asked what the Mexicans were going to do in the middle of the desert, one dick said, "Don't worry. They ain't human."

The bulls' domain extended to the jungles as well as the trains. Many a hobo camp was dismantled by bull raiding parties who shot up cooking utensils, burned clothes, and tore down homemade shacks.

Some 'boes reduced the train jumper-bull conflict to something of an applied science. The chances of being caught between two points on a railroad line, so the hobo handicapping theory went, depended on the distance, the number of separate tracks between the two points, the number of daily runs, and the track mileage patrolled by each agent in the road's police department. The Illinois Central was one of the most inviting to the jumping fraternity. To arrive at the actual odds of being nabbed, the distance from Chicago to Cairo (363) was multiplied by the number of tracks (2), multiplied again by the average daily run of trains (35), then divided by the actual track mileage patrolled by each agent (100). A train jumper on the Illinois Central had the odds in his favor, 254 to 1.

But fanciful formulas aside, the 'boes took the bull chal-

lenge with deadly seriousness and much bitterness. Of the
Jeff Carrs of the world, one hobo wrote, "Here's to the dawn
of the day when the world will be rid of the greatest mon-
strosity of modern times, the R.R. Bull. And when he dies
he will have to have an airship to go up into hell, if there be
such a place; and should he make it, if the devil and his family have any self-respect in their make-up, they will tell him
to beat it and start a Hell of his own."

When train jumpers were able to outwit the crews and the
Jeff Carrs, it was manna to the fraternity ego. Some of the
stories of the great con jobs made the rounds of jungle fires
for many years. One such story: An engineer stops a passenger train near Centralia, Illinois, in 1885 after seeing a man
standing over a body sprawled on the tracks. When a crowd
from the train reaches the scene, the man on his feet explains
that he had seen the dead man on the tracks and wanted to
stop the train before it mangled him. "Why didn't you pull
him off the track?" asks the conductor logically. "I couldn't
be hired to touch a dead body," replies the stranger. But just
a minute! One of the crowd discovers that the body still has
life in it. "I think that he's taken poison," remarks the
stranger, "and laid down here to make sure work of it. If you
are a mind to take him to Centralia I'll kind o' rub him into
life and get a doctor to pump him out." The engineer orders
the man placed in the baggage car. Concerned passengers
then raise seven dollars for the poor unfortunate and give it
to the stranger for the man's care. Just before the train
reaches Centralia, two figures leap from the baggage car and,
with a couple of whoops and yells, run across a field.

The 'bo hunt brought financial rewards for many brakemen and conductors. Instead of ditching captured prey, the
crewmen extracted "'bo money," tribute for continuing to
ride. Many railway employees counted on such extra cash to
boost meager wages and some shacks were not above locking

trespassers in sealed cars until money or other goods were forthcoming. On some of the lines the crew might do business with the jumpers for a flask of booze or a few plugs of tobacco. But most often they demanded hard cash. One 'bo who had been a boomer shack himself in earlier years confessed, "It was against the rules. It was against the law. It was against the precepts of humanity and brotherly love to collect 'bo money. I certainly got my share of it." The tramp writer Josiah Flynt revealed that the late nineteenth-century rate was about ten cents a hundred miles or twenty cents for a full night's ride. Inflation, however, shot prices ten times higher in the next few years. In the early 1900s "a dollar a division" was the usual fare. The penalty for nonpayment was often a busted jaw and an ignominious flight to the cinders.

Even if a jumper successfully eluded the train dicks and the crews and swung aboard without disaster, he still had to face the possibility of a bad ride. 'Boes told of picking ancient, poorly lubricated boxcars that spent more time off the tracks than on and bounced the temporary occupants like rubber balls. Jumpers learned quickly the art of squatting bronco-riding style to absorb the shocks of the repeated jolts. But a bad ride was the least the train jumper could expect. Prominently pictured in a *Life* magazine article in the 1930s is a grisly photo of the body of a jumper completely severed in two equal pieces.

The railroad was both demon and friend. It gave life to the hobo existence, offered opportunity, adventure, and escape. But it left in its wake thousands who found, instead of a pathway to the Big Rock Candy Mountain, a barbarous, violent death. Hoboes were dumped on the tracks from hopper cars when insecurely fastened doors opened; dissected by boxcar doors that unexpectedly closed; crushed by shifting, loose loads in gondolas; suffocated in reefers when the trapdoors to the compartments accidentally locked; jolted off blind platforms; rolled off the decks of both freight cars and passenger cars; mashed attempting to swing on; squashed on the roadbeds after falling from the rods; and shot by bulls and fellow roaming stiffs. A tramp once told the sociologist John J. McCook of seeing a man run over by one train as he was about to hop another. "When we fall off," the tramp gruesomely quipped, "there is a fight between the towns as to which shall furnish the box."

The chief of the Pennsylvania Railroad police reported that in the years 1899–1902 nearly 2,000 train jumpers were killed on that line's tracks and nearly 500 suffered injuries that resulted in major amputation. These figures applied to only 2,000 miles of track out of the 182,000 miles in the United States. At the National Conference of Charities and Corrections in June 1907, railroad officials representing more than half the total railway mileage in the United States claimed that the number of trespassers killed annually on the trains exceeded the number of passengers and trainmen killed. Reports from railroad companies to the Interstate Commerce Commission showed that in the ten-year period ending in December 1908, more than 47,000 railroad trespassers had lost their lives. It was, the officials noted, a slaughter.

President James J. Hill of the Great Northern wrote, "Hundreds of idle men infest empty cars . . . during the summer months. . . . They get on or off trains while in motion, and some suffer in life and limb. Others fall off while asleep. It would be difficult to gather reliable statistics on this point, because a large percentage of the tramps reported as killed on the railroads are really murdered. Men returning from the harvest fields with their wages are killed for their money by their more vicious and criminal fellows, the body is flung from the train while in motion and the reported death by railroad casualty is actually a case of homicide." Hill didn't mention those killed by his and the other railroads' own police. Not all the victims of violent death along the tracks were train jumpers; some were factory workmen and women and children who lived near the railroads. But most were stiffs who had either fallen or had been pushed under the grinding wheels.

But even with the horror and pain, the railroad was the life force of the American hobo. Down every track, in the cars, along the sidings, in the jungles by the water tanks, the threats waited—the bulls and shacks, the killer wheels, the cold and the jails. But most of the thousands who challenged the road could look back with Harry Kemp, the tramp poet, with some hauteur at having taken up the challenge:

> *I've decked the tops of flying cars*
> *That leaped across the night;*
> *The long and level coaches skimmed*
> *Low, like a swallow's flight.*

> *Close to the sleet-bit blinds I've clung*
> *Rocking on and on;*
> *All night I've crouched in empty cars*
> *That rode into the dawn.*

> *Seeing the ravelled edge of life*
> *In jails, on rolling freights*
> *And learning rough and ready ways*
> *From rough and ready mates.*

VAG LAWS AND BOODLE JAILS

From his father's farm near Osage, Iowa, in the 1870s, Hamlin Garland saw an invasion of tramps at harvest time, an invasion that vanished almost as mysteriously as it had first appeared. "A few of them had been soldiers," Garland wrote, "others were the errant sons of poor farmers and rough mechanics of older states, migrating for the adventure of it." In O. Henry's story "Whistling Dick's Christmas Stocking," a wealthy planter baron talks of tramps swarming up and down the Mississippi River, overrunning New Orleans. "They won't work," he laments, "they defy my overseers and they make friends with my dogs."

Newspapers in the 1870s began to blaze with stories about tramp depredations—train hijackings, robberies, gangs of rioting desperadoes, pitched battles between vigilante groups and hordes of Hunlike invaders. Much of this was hyperbole; much of it was not. As numerous railroad employees, farmers, and town officials testified, the menace of the train-jumping legions was not mere fantasy.

In Iowa, 300 tramps took over a train. In Rock Island, Illinois, city officials called on war veterans to protect the city from what they regarded as a tramp plague; in Moline, the fire department was armed to the teeth to ward off an invasion of the land pirates; at Elkhart, Indiana, the rail yards became a kind of convention site as hundreds of homeless, unemployed men bedded down by the tracks waiting for freights. Shootings were rampant, the *Railroad Gazette* reported in 1876: "Yesterday a west-bound train on the Toledo, Wabash Western Railway was bounced at Chapin Station by about 100 of these gentry; the train crew persuaded them out of the caboose, and they then got on top of the train and commenced throwing coal at the train men. A shot gun was procured and leveled at them, but failed to go off; then one of the tramps drew a revolver and shot the brakeman who had the gun, wounding him in the leg. After this they captured a train at Roodhouse on Chicago and Alton Railroad and forced the conductor to take them up to Jacksonville."

Railroad officials grumbled that the trespassers were steal-

ing and destroying millions of dollars each year on the
trains. Train jumpers, they complained, broke open boxes
and cases of merchandise to search for small, compact valuable goods which they could carry away; the rest of the con-
tents was thrown out or damaged. One railroad worker in
New Mexico in 1884 despaired that the country was crawl-
ing with tramps and that the pestilence was getting worse
every day. "You see," the railroad man noted, "the country
was different before the railroads got in. Then it took a small
fortune to get down here; stage fare was fifteen cents a mile,
and every one who came had capital enough to start a ranch
or go prospecting . . . the tramp had no show in the old stage
days." In July 1877 the chief of the Massachusetts detective
force sent two of his men to live incognito among tramps
roaming around the Berkshire hills. Their report: the unemployed nomads despised work, were criminals, and were a
grievous threat to the entire Massachusetts citizenry. One
writer in *Scribner's Monthly* characterized the wandering
train jumper and his lofty station in society in these terms:
"He has no more rights than the sow that wallows in the
gutter, or the lost dog that hovers around the city squares.
He is no more to be consulted, in his wishes or his will, in
the settlement of the question as to what is to be done with
him, than if he were a bullock in a corral." One railroad magazine declared that the loathsome roving gangs were spreading depravity and a contagion of immorality and laziness,
pollution and litter, and blatant pauperism. The *Railroad
Gazette* reported almost gleefully in June 1877 that one of
the vile creatures had received his rightful punitive reward.
As a stiff was standing on the New York Central track near
Amsterdam, New York, throwing stones at a passing
express train, he was crunched by a locomotive coming from
the opposite direction.

The specter of the tramp threat in the late nineteenth

century stirred heated demands in public journals, state legislatures, and town meetings, and the heat was mostly on the
side of whipping the beasts into shape. As enthusiasts eagerly combed old English precedents for dealing with the
hordes of unemployed, they discovered certain "tramp"
laws enacted some 300 years earlier. For the first offense of
begging, the offender had been driven back to his birthplace
and forced to work; for the second, the gristle of his right
ear had been lopped off; and for the third, the incorrigible
felon had been executed. Some hard-liners probably saw a
modest solution to the tramp onslaught in Washington Irving's 1809 burlesque, *The History of New York*. Irving described the gibbet by which Governor William the Testy
dangled vagrants and beggers: "It is incredible how the little
Governor chuckled at beholding caitiff vagrants and sturdy
beggars thus swinging by the crupper, and cutting antic
gambols in the air. He had a thousand pleasantries and
mirthful conceits to utter upon those occasions. He called
them his dandelions, his wild-fowl, his high-flyers, his
spread-eagles, his goshawks, his scarecrows, and finally, his
gallows-birds."

If local and state officials did not opt for stocks, slashed
eyelids, branded foreheads, slit noses, thumbscrews, whip-
pings, and ear loppings in the manner of old England (or for
the gibbet in the manner of William the Testy), they did
begin to take energetic legislative steps to end the influx of
jobless wayfarers on the trains. The Pennsylvania vagrancy
law passed in 1876 defined tramps and vagrants as "all persons who shall come from any place without this Commonwealth to any place within; and shall be found loitering or
residing therein, and shall follow no labor, trade, occupation,
or business, and have no visible means of subsistence, and
can give no reasonable account of themselves." Such persons
were to be arrested and set to work for not less than thirty

days or more than six months. The Delaware tramp law of 1879 simply defined an offender as any person wandering about without home or job and provided for a sentence from one to thirty days. States all across the country passed similar hurried, panicked, ill-defined statutes. In two southern states the legislatures established sale at auction as a penalty and blacks who witnessed drifters being sold off for periods of work must have had jarring memories of a too recent past.

A typical court proceeding for a man arrested for vagrancy was often close to the following:

> *Judge:* Why are you in town?
> *Accused:* I'm trying to find a job.
> *Judge:* Where are you headed?
> *Accused:* New York.
> *Judge:* Why?
> *Accused:* To look for work.
> *Judge:* How much money do you have?
> *Accused:* I'm broke.
> *Judge:* What are you going to do tonight?
> *Accused:* I don't know.
> *Judge:* You are a vagrant. Sentence: seven days.

If pauperism represented to the Calvinist mind a badge of sin, the vagrancy laws provided a means of swift retribution. Men were daily run out of town or imprisoned for no other offense than being penniless. States tried various methods of incarceration. In West Virginia the overseers of the poor were charged with caring for the wanderers; Missouri, Rhode Island, Connecticut, Michigan, and New Jersey sent vags to almshouses and workhouses; Massachusetts, New York, Maryland, Illinois, and New Jersey committed many tramps to jails, penitentiaries, and houses of correction. In Kentucky the tramp could be sold into servitude for up to twelve months; in Virginia and New Mexico the government herded the tramps to work on public projects or hired them out. Tramp legislation obviously lacked integration and consistency. It was this lack of a national policy that mired the tramp problem in contradiction, confusion, and anarchy.

For some of the tramp marauders and thugs, the jail sentences were well earned. For the many stiffs who were on the road honestly looking for work, however, the sentences were anything but just. One train jumper who was thrown in jail wrote, "We were locked up in an unsanitary cell with the small windows sealed up half way with cement; twelve men in a cell nine feet by sixteen; no sanitary arrangements outside of a common tin water bucket—sleeping on the floor—no bedding or benches whatever. With the exception of two women and two men awaiting trial, all the prisoners are freight riders—shanghaied to make a living for a bunch of cheap grafters and crook officials. None of us considered we had committed a crime—arrested for doing nothing—on our way doing the work of the country."

Capturing rail nomads could be profitable for enterprising law-enforcement officials. One freight rider explained: "The sheriff gets a dollar a day for feeding the boes. He gives them about twelve cents' worth of food . . . we got thirty days and were turned loose after spending three days in cells where they had lice at least three years old, if size counts for anything. The prisoners do three days out of thirty and the whole thirty days is charged to the State—twenty-seven days' clear profit for the crooks." American boodle jails, the stiffs called them. Will J. Quirke, hobo bard, wrote in 1919:

> Early every morning the Sheriff comes around,
> He gives us rotten herring that weighs a quarter pound;
> With coffee like tobacco juice and bread that's hard and
>   stale,
> And this is the way they feed us boes in Cecil County Jail.

Local vengeance, unleashed against the criminal tramp, indiscriminately wrecked lives of many other men of the road. If a stiff were picked up in Houston for vagrancy, he was given a mug shot and paraded before a lineup. In Corpus Christi, the penalty for sleeping in a boxcar in the yards of the Southern Pacific was seventeen days in the county workhouse. In one innovative jail in southern Florida, the jobless were treated to a small dose of current from an electrically wired seat. Many wanderers arrested as vags in Florida could truthfully say they had survived an electric chair.

Sometimes entire communities found sport in tormenting beggars. In one Iowa community a black-and-blue vagabond recounted one memorable afternoon: "They ketches four of us and makes us run the ga'ntlet, and believe me I run. The natives stands on each side for a quarter of a mile or more. . . . They hit us wit' stones and whips. . . . Some guy caught me wit' a rock here where you see this bump. . . . I'll bet there was two hundred men there, an' a dozen women." In 1894 a Sacramento vigilante committee regularly swept into hobo camps, took mug shots of the inhabitants, and drove them farther out of town. In Los Angeles, the 'boes might have considered their Sacramento compatriots fortunate. "Every afternoon," one Los Angeles *Herald* reporter wrote, "the clashing of chains on Second Street, in front of the police station . . . the members of the chain gang—poorly fed, ragged, and dirty—appear to the full view of the tourist. Little children stand in droves and watch the poor fellows as they lift the balls and chains and stagger, half exhausted, into their squalid cells to spend the night."

Elizabeth, New Jersey, should have received an award for ingenuity in dealing with the tramp invasion. If the vile creatures were akin to rats, as many of the newspaper articles suggested, why not deal with the pests in the traditional manner—thus, the notorious "tramp trap." Placed invitingly on a switch of the Pennsylvania Railroad outside Elizabeth, a solitary boxcar, doors ajar, beckoned to weary roamers. At about ten o'clock each night the trap was usually occupied by at least a few catches and the police had merely to spring the doors and hustle the boys off to the station. A few hours later the trap had usually landed a few more. Until word of this tactic reverberated along the train-riding communication vine, the trap was an enormous success.

One Delanco, New Jersey, constable went a few steps further. He chained tramps to trees in the village square. The experiment was notably popular both for the swarms of mosquitoes from nearby lowlands who feasted on the defenseless stiffs staked on the trees and for the townspeople who quickly had fewer and fewer tramps. "After one visit here," the constable remarked, "lots of them never come back a second time."

Hobo Bill, a crusty, articulate track veteran who now travels around the country in a small camper, remembers Texas as an especially rugged host for him and his kindred souls. A 'bo, naive about the ways of the Lone Star, might saunter up to a police station to inquire about shelter possibilities and find himself on a rock pile for months. As in Los Angeles, the sight of wretched, demoralized homeless men manacled to convicted felons was common in Texas and a few other states. In much of the public mind, of course, the common legal fate of the vagrant and the thief meant a common lineage—they were all criminals.

The *Hobo News* charged in 1919 that the vagrancy laws in the various states were, in effect, creating legalized slavery benefiting cheap contractors and road builders. Thousands of homeless drifters and migratory workers, arrested for hopping freights or for merely hanging around without a job, found themselves on chain gangs and turpentine farms. Thousands of miles of roads in the United States were built

by crews of hobo laborers, many of whom were broken by
the punishment and died. With few friends, no political influence or legal protection, the 'boes were easy marks for
broadly worded and constructed statutes which made the
hobo life-style a crime.

But the effort through the vag laws to rid the country of
the tramp invasion was generally a failure. The numbers of
men roaming the country in boxcar berths and on the rods
continued to grow. In the halcyon days of the hobo, when
each train rolling toward the lumber camps and berry fields
carried droves of workers, when several hundred of them
covered each incoming freight car to the harvest fields like
roosting birds, the laws against train jumping and vagrancy
became ineffective and, in some cases, something of a joke.
One 'bo remembered hearing from the windows of a jail cell
the sweet refrains of "Hallelujah, I'm a Bum" filling the
morning air of a small western town. As more stiffs began to
swell the numbers, as the jail reached capacity and most of
the faces in the town turned eerily unfamiliar to the embattled sheriff, the captives suddenly became captors. The prisoners not only were released but enjoyed a hearty breakfast
at town expense. The cocky train jumpers then had an im-
promptu meeting and passed a resolution that their exit from
the city limits could only be accomplished after each received a generous slice of pumpkin pie, a resolution quickly
accepted by town authorities.

As the number of road wanderers increased and the jails
bulged with homeless men, many town officials concluded
that the vag laws were not only ineffective but extraordinar-
ily expensive for local governments. Providing room and
board in jails in the winter months, many judges began to
growl, was like throwing Br'er Rabbit into the briarpatch.
The best solution, they decided, was to kick the pests out of
town. A typical punishment for train jumping after the turn

of the century was that meted out to a hobo named Wallace by a Duluth, Minnesota, judge in 1908: "Ten days in the workhouse with the condition that the sentence be suspended if he would leave town immediately." The Associated Charities of Kansas reported in the same year that a popular procedure involved the arrest of the stiff, forced work on the rock pile for a few days, an inattentive guard who invited escape, and the intended disappearance of the prisoner. As the number of illegal train riders spurred visions of overcrowded jails, jammed court dockets, and depleted city and town treasuries, local officials, although continuing to jail vagrants, began simply to kick most homeless men on their way. Judicial purists might have pointed out that no judge or policeman in the country had the right of deportation; yet many rail stiffs were marched out of town after town by officials anxious to pass the problem somewhere on down the line. Inadvertently, of course, this tactic contributed to and sustained the road traffic. If a 'bo wandered into town in the morning in a genuine search for a job, he might find himself marching on the rails before sundown.

Railroad officials began to complain bitterly that local law-enforcement agencies were becoming increasingly lax in dealing with train jumpers. James J. Hill remarked that when justices ordered vagrants to leave town, the trespassing problem was only exacerbated: "When all neighborhoods are doing the same thing, the community receives exactly as much refuse as it gets rid of." The *Utica Observer* in 1911 gave an account of a trial of two men, one an unemployed plumber, caught jumping a passenger train. The newspaper account was reprinted in the *Railway Age Gazette* as an example of local jurisprudence actually thwarting the efforts of the railroads to keep ticketless passengers off the trains. "Judge O'Connor's eyes brightened with happy recollections," the account revealed. " 'They showed pluck and perseverance,' said the judge. 'I like that kind of spirit. I remember that I was kicked off a train six times by railroad detectives in Chicago when I was broke in that city one time. . . . A plumber is like a burglar—if he can get three or four good jobs a year he doesn't have to work the rest of the time.' 'I'm looking for those jobs now,' said the man.' 'You deserve a show, then,' said the judge. Both men received suspended sentences." Irate railroad officials pointed out that while they were organizing larger and larger police forces to attack the rail-trespassing menace, local magistrates were becoming more and more reluctant to prosecute. The judges were in a sense acting in league with the criminals.

Town officials had a logical response. Commissioners of Beaver, Lawrence, and Mercer counties in Pennsylvania echoed the sentiments of many of their brethren when they declared that their county treasuries would not foot the bill for the care and feeding of men arrested for hopping freights. The railroad industry had created the problem in the first place, the local officials argued, and should bear the expense and burden of solving the problem. The impasse was formidable—the local authorities insisting that railroads should pay the bills for jailing the prisoners, the railroads insisting that the town and county governments enforce their own vagrancy laws more forcefully.

The railroad companies and local officials never did reach any kind of satisfactory accord in dealing with the train-jumping problem. Their only mutual agreement seemed to be that the tramp and hobo pestilence was as hard to eradicate as rats and roaches.

Meanwhile, thousands of men continued to be bounced in and out of boodle jails and workhouses, and kicked out of one town after another. As one hobo wrote, "Men are driven almost to the point of distraction by big beef-eating bulls and bullying judges; vagged if they walk the roads; hired out to farmers who don't want to pay wages; building roads for states that want to save taxes; branded as criminals for riding in old empty cars; blamed for goods stolen off trains by shacks and Sears-Roebuck detectives."

The conflict between the train jumpers and their antagonists, the railroads and the towns, was steeped in irony. Towns in the wheat belt, for example, desperately needed the labor of the itinerant workers, and the railroad companies stood to suffer severe losses if the grain districts they serviced did not receive the necessary numbers of harvest hands. Certainly no public authority in a grain-growing district needing the muscle of hobo labor was about to prosecute vigorously the train-jumping activity during harvest seasons. "In harvest time," one 'bo remarked in the 1920s, "we are begged to come to town by the Chamber of Commerce. We stay until the harvest is over and then we are chased out of town by the cops." As Seebohm Rowntree, the English cocoa manufacturer, put it, "Men are thrown aside as you chuck an orange peel after you have sucked the orange."

A few did cry in the wilderness for the rights of the drifters. Populist Governor Lorenzo Lewelling of Kansas issued a proclamation in 1893 that said in part that the Constitution guaranteed all individuals the freedom to move freely from place to place without interference and that the vagrancy laws, classing penniless individuals with criminals, were inhuman. His manifesto, which later became known as the "Tramp Circular," was anything but popularly received. If newspaper editorialists were not taking his notion as a preposterous joke, they were attacking the Governor for consorting with lunatic anarchists and other left-wing radicals.

With the 1894 depression sucking jobs from workers across the country, another spokesman for the roving population emerged. A young Ohioan named Jacob Coxey organized a mass protest march of unemployed to Washington. The demand was for Congress to issue some five million dollars in greenbacks to finance road building and other public projects to put the jobless to work. At the same time, Charles T. Kelly, a young San Francisco printer, organized another group in the West to join Coxey in the march to the nation's capital. It was this contingent of the army that Jack London joined in Omaha, Nebraska, and from which many of the London stories of the road were born. The Socialist Eugene Debs, attempting to marshal support for the marchers before the Railway Workers' convention, declared, "From almost every center of population in all of the land, from mountain and valley, from hill and dale, from abandoned mine and silent factory, shop and forge—they come and tramp to the muffled drum—funeral march of their throbbing hearts. The cry is, 'On to Washington,' where, on the marble steps of the nation's capitol, in their rags, and barefooted, they would petition Congress to enact laws whereby they might perpetuate their wretched existence by toil."

The march of the unemployed brought no relief. Federal legislators, railroad officials, and local government leaders were not ready to believe with Washington Gladden, theologian and social philosopher, that the tramp and hobo phenomenon was a result of economic determinism. They were more ready to accept the ideas espoused by the popular preacher Russell Cornwell. Every poor person in the country, Cornwell taught, was made poor by his own shortcomings and by God's punishment for sin. To give sympathy and, indeed, alms to train-jumping tramps and vags was frustrating the divine will and purpose of God. No dusty, smoke-swathed stiff just off a rattler ever got a setdown at Russell Cornwell's back door. Cornwell echoed the sentiments of other antibenevolence spokesmen who insisted that government should maintain a laissez-faire stance in the tramp matter except, of course, for the punishment of crimes.

A long, bitter article in *Railroad Man's Magazine* in 1917, attacking the drifter class, declared, "This human parasite is as much a part and parcel of the American railroad institution as ties, stations, and water tanks." If the characterization was emotionally charged, the basic assertion was correct. The society of road vagabonds had grown with the railroads; learned its operations and intricacies and language; traveled to all parts of the nation over its spreading arteries; faced its challenges of loneliness and violence; fought and frustrated its police; provided labor for the industries it serviced; experienced the joys of the freedom it offered; and suffered the injuries and death it wrung from the unfortunate. If the road claimed the lives of thousands, if the vag laws and the boodle jails destroyed others, the railroad remained the salient part of the hobo life. "I pulled my cap down over my eyes," an old hobo song told, "And walked on down the tracks; Then I caught an empty car; And never did look back."

3/ *John McCook and the Peripatetic Aristocracy*

THE FACES in the photographs stare almost without expression: five gentlemen of the road, each with a sporty bowler and a black, rumpled suit, strike somewhat debonair poses; two veteran train jumpers display their technique of riding the rods; more than a hundred transients crowd an East Side New York mission-house chapel to await sermons and sandwiches; half-dressed men sprawl on cots and on the floor around a stove in a seven-cent New York lodging house; a dozen jungling stiffs and a dog surround a four-gallon kettle of mulligan; tramps under hay in a Hartford barn are awakened by police at 1:00 A.M. to be escorted to jail; men in a wayfarers' lodge in Boston take a bath, one with his bowler still in place. These and other photographs are a gallery of Americans caught up in a world on society's fringes—train jumpers, shovel and gutter bums, winos, tomato-can vags, simple beggars and gifted grafters, the homeless and alienated, the indigent and debilitated. This was not the world of the man who commissioned the photographs, the clergyman and college professor who for over two decades made an exhaustive investigation of that world—John J. McCook.

One of the fifteen "Fighting McCooks" who served in the Civil War, John McCook was ordained a deacon in the Episcopal church in 1866, became a rector of a parish in East Hartford, Connecticut, and in 1883 joined the faculty of Trinity College as an instructor of Latin and, later, as professor of modern languages. Active in local civic affairs, McCook began to voice concern over the amount of municipal money being drained off for alms, and in 1890 was named to chair a committee to investigate the distribution of

funds to paupers. It was the chairmanship of this alms committee that led the austere professor into an absorbing study
of the transient world—from flophouses to jungles, from
railroad yards to saloons.

McCook's fascination with the subject was almost imme-
diate. He began to trail the rail-riding community with zeal,
interviewing homeless wanderers in the streets, gathering
information from police and reformatory officials, visiting
almshouses and public baths. From the wayfarers' lodges
where they slept to the boxcars where they rode, the professor sought them out. He drew up a questionnaire which elic-
ited more than 1,300 responses from tramps and hoboes
across the country. He photographed them; sampled the various brands of rotgut liquor they consumed; ate their mulligan stew; and watched police make raids on their hangouts.
He dogged them for hours at a time, jotting down their
haunts and plotting maps of their wanderings. The gentlemen scholar and clergyman of Hartford thus got to know
very well Providence Bob, Philadelphia Shorty, and other
knights of the rail.

McCook's investigations compelled many homeless stiffs
to pour out their stories in great detail, as they never had before to an outsider. In Marshall, Texas, one "Bob" penned a
twelve-page letter to the professor, explaining that he had
run away from home at age twelve, fallen in with bands of
marauding thieves, done time in reformatories and prisons,
escaped, and permanently joined the ranks of the train-
jumping community. Determined never to return to con-
finement, Bob carried an "emergency pill" of cyanide in case
of capture. As he lounged in the woods that he called "Hotel
de Bum," with an old mule nosing around his feet, and with
friends Denver Shine, Oregon Bob, and Colorado Slim
nearby, Bob wrote to McCook, "Your tramp found his greatest pleasure in the beauties of nature. . . . I have seen most of

the scenery of the west, but never could thoroughly enjoy it, unless I could feel tucked away, somewhere next to my skin, a wad of that green stuff that means good food, attention and all the creature comforts."

Another wanderer wrote McCook, "I often in day time, nice days, get into the woods in some secluded spot, lay down in the shade of some friendly tree and sleep from two or three hours, sometimes longer. . . . I often think God intended man to live as the Indians used to—all the land common property. What happy times if we was all in the Woods together."

In May 1893, the professor handed six postal cards to a tramp named Connecticut Fatty and asked that he send back to Hartford accounts of his travels. That single gesture by McCook was perhaps the most fortuitous in all of his work. Although Fatty never did report back his road exploits as McCook had hoped, one of the cards was given to a roaming mushfaker and Civil War veteran named William Aspinwall. On May 18, 1893, Aspinwall wrote to McCook from Jewett City, Connecticut, "Kind Sir I received this postal card from a gentleman of leisure I met on my Route. He said you was Seeking information from the fraternity Haut Beaus. I suppose you are writing some Book now if you want any points on this kind of a life I can give them to you." And he did. Aspinwall began to send long letters from various small-town post offices describing in intimate detail his frustrations and small triumphs on the road. McCook sent return letters to post offices that Aspinwall expected to reach weeks later. The correspondence with "Roving Bill" laid the foundation for much of McCook's investigative work. The professor wrote later, "I have a file of letters from him more than seven inches thick, ranging from a page to sixty pages, covering a majority of the States of the Union, describing with the utmost particularity, and with a candor at times quite Rabelaisian, his occupations, his leisure, his amours, his potations, his sensations, his religious views and his political and economic faith, his earnings, his expenditures . . ."

In his rambling travels Aspinwall, essentially a loner who avoided hobo camps, refused to ask for alms and spent periods of time in veterans homes. He also took an occasional job, especially in woolen mills. On the hoof more than most men of the road, he did flip occasional freights and wrote of several harrowing escapes from injury. He expressed great disgust with homosexual activity he witnessed. He often mentioned his frustrating lapses into periods of intemperance. But most of all he talked of the freedom of the vagabond life and the pleasures of nature.

In 1901–02, McCook published a series of nine articles in *The Independent* on the Aspinwall letters. In frequent speaking engagements, the professor read long passages from the remarkable letters of his roaming correspondent— "Leaves from the Diary of a Tramp," he called them. One of the letters talked at length about the classes of wanderers:

> There is several classes of tramps or Haut Beaus. I can make about three out of them with occasionally a woman. There is 1st the Harmless Tramp that tramps because he has no home, no Friends and got on the road from Drink and then No. 2 is Fakers and Mush Fakers, Mechanics and others on the Tramp hunting work, and some of the finest mechanicks in the country, comprising all trades, get on the road by spending their money too liberal and Partly from drink and get down and ashamed to ask for a Job, and good fellows they are, will divide the last nickel with you or the last Biscuit. There appears to be a kind of Brotherly feeling amongst this Class, but they have no use for Class No. 3 as they are composed of ex-Convicts, Jails Birds and Regular Dead Beats. There is some mean Haut Beaus that will venture to do anything—insult Women, steal and fire Barns, Can't be trusted. This makes it bad for an Honest man as the Public thinks they are all Chips of the same block, but

far from it. Just as much difference in the Classes as there is
in the Classes of societies in a Citty, or a Vilage. . . . It is the
last Class that has all the signs and Camps and patronizes
the Poor Houses, Jails, &c. They manage to get some
money by stealing or Begging and Buy Alcohall, dilute it in
Watter and drink that. They call it Alca', or Booze and
other names. . . . I have seen several women on the tramp,
but generally very low down creatures. The boys call them
Bags, old Bags. A man along with a Bag don't stand very
high in Haut Beau society. Framers are called Rubes. When
a Bum goes to a house and gets a lunch they call it Hand
out, Lump, Soup, Slop, &c.

Forty-eight years old when he began writing to McCook,
Aspinwall was proud of his road exploits. "I think I can say
without doubt," he wrote, "that I have tramped and Roamed
about more in my life than any man of my age in America
went through all the vicisitudes and Hardships it is Posible
for a Human to stand and live . . ."

The itinerant umbrella mender and the reverend/sociolo-
gist never met personally. But the letters from the road kept
coming—from New York and Ohio, Providence and Pitts-
burgh, from New Hampshire to Mexico, from big cities to
railroad junctions. They talked of tramp vernacular and
tramp song; yeggs and their prushins; of boiling up and panhandling; of women tramps; of economic depression and
personal depression; of politics and graft; of swarms of train
jumpers covering trains like bees over hives.

In a letter of June 6, 1897, Aspinwall enclosed a photo-
graph of himself taken at McCook's request in Bennington,
Vermont. Standing appropriately in front of a pastoral
mural, the stubbled veteran of the pike and rail stood un-
smiling, with an air of nobility, his umbrella-mending kit
hanging from one shoulder, his pipe cocked to the side. Until
shortly before his death in November 1921 at the State Soldiers' Home in Erie County, Ohio, Roving Bill kept up the

letter-writing relationship with McCook. The correspondence was a treasure of information for the Hartford professor and his sociological investigation. In one of his more re-
flective passages Aspinwall wrote:

> The inhabitants of this earth is divided into two masses one
> party does the work the other the theoretical part of it. The-
> ory will not do alone but theory and actual practice will as-
> simulate sometimes I believe from my own personal ob-
> servation wich has been extensive that the poor are much
> more temperate than many of their critics would have us
> believe. If mere doing is to get us praise what laudable and
> industrious men were Alexander and Bonapart. the seeds
> they sowed were evil. It is all verry well for the . . . author
> or member of Congress to abuse us as idle drifters and
> drunken bums and hobos You must remember our vocation
> is somewhat exciting, but not pleasant ennobling nor renu-
> merative Often I have heard proffessional men say what
> does the hobo know about work. About as much or more
> than the proffesional men at the same time. . . . It is easy to
> tell a hobo to go to work and be industrious and contented
> in that walk of life to wich Providence has called him But
> it would be neither easy nor pleasant to take his place and
> show him how it should be done, and I tell you frankly I
> believe that if Providence called a Senator or a Bishop a
> Profs to do the Hobo act Providence would have to use a
> trumpet or the gentlemen would not hear.

If the Aspinwall letters were an intimate, personal source,
the questionnaires provided a broad range of statistical information. In 1891, McCook devised the form which he
hoped would provide insight into the origins, habits, and
health of the homeless vagabonds. He asked questions about
occupation, previous employment, length of time on the
road, desire for work, incidence of venereal disease, marital
status, temperance, criminal record, voting habits, literacy,
and other general questions on age, color, citizenship, religion, and real and assumed names. McCook sent letters to

mayors of forty cities asking their help in carrying out the investigation. He enclosed with the letters pads of the questionnaires which were to be distributed through social agencies in various areas of the country. The response was surprisingly full. Some of the answers on the forms were obviously tongue-in-cheek or exaggerated, but most appeared to be honest. They conveyed both the pathos and humor typical of many road knights. From one William Smith, forty-two-year-old white American: occupation, "gentleman"; hit the road, he says, the moment he could walk; does not intend to work that day or any other; health good but stomach empty; has had syphilis and the itch and has been hospitalized nine times; was married five times and doesn't know whether any children resulted; drinks as much as he can; has no religion. From one Christopher Bentley, a native Englishman: a musician by trade; took to the road only five weeks ago looking for work but claims to be a "natural bum"; has bad health including bouts with venereal disease; stayed in an almshouse the last winter; sleeps almost anywhere; is intemperate and has been arrested five times for drunkenness; plays the piano in various whorehouses.

McCook received surprising cooperation from police officials and, in more than one instance, something of a thoughtful examination of the tramp and hobo question. From the New York City Police Department came this assessment: "The Tramp is as much a product of civilization as are any and all of the arts and sciences. Density of population, the disposition to herd together in large cities, tenement occupation, the tightly drawn lines of social distinction and contact, the affinity of money for itself whereby the rich constantly grow richer and the poor poorer, the combinations of capital in every conceivable way, producing and reproducing at will without demand, and refusing to produce if profit accrue therefrom, the legislation, State and Na-

tional, effected by greed and monopolistic desire—all tend to
make the Tramp, and, like the famed Frankenstein, when
once created he cannot be unmade."

From these responses and the many others he received,
McCoo) began to draw a number of conclusions. In 1893 he
published an article in *The Forum* entitled "A Tramp Cen-
sus and Its Revelations," a work which was the first important statistical study of homelessness made in the United
States. In this and other articles, McCook developed a portrait of the tramp and hobo population. The majority of this
"Peripatetic Aristocracy," as he called them, had been
tradesmen or artisans such as weavers, shoemakers, stone-
cutters, machinists, and masons; an overwhelming propor-
tion were single men who had never been married, although
there were a few "Magpies" and "Petticoat Bums" on the
road; most were under forty years of age, with approximately 5 percent under twenty; most were white north-
erners; most were confessed heavy drinkers or alcoholics, a
fact confirming the observation of one of the vagabond tip-
plers that "Where there is honey there are bees; where there
is beer there is bums"; approximately 10 percent admitted
they suffered from venereal disease, a figure that McCook
and officials of hospitals and detention centers suspected was
a bit low; 90 percent were literate.

Some were obviously hardened yeggs, parasites feasting
on the public as well as fellow road nomads. McCook called
them "predatory, bold and violent; land pirates with no
Captain Kidd to control them; merry men of Sherwood Forest without the redeeming chivalry of Robin Hood and the
rude piety of Friar Tuck."

A majority had never voted, although, for a handout, some
had sold their votes. "I would not sell my vote at the Polls of
a Presidential election," one stiff told McCook, "I think too
much of the principles." One claimed that he had voted

eight times in one New York municipal election and went away with sixteen dollars. A detective, when told of the man's claim, said the story was exaggerated—not the venal voting but the payoffs. "He never got anything like that," the detective assured the Reverend.

Most of those who responded to the questionnaire were born in the United States. When sociologists mingled with the casual labor class twenty years later, many men swinging bindles on passing freights spoke Lithuanian, Italian, or Polish. But even in later years the man of the road was most often a native-born American.

McCook saw a link between the tramp and hobo population and the eddies of labor strikes, unemployment, industrial panics, and general economic malaise. The first employees laid off, McCook concluded, were usually alcoholics; then single men—those with few family ties and little self-discipline. Many of these men chose to hit the road in search of a job and in search of emotional relief.

As he totaled the figures from the piles of questionnaires and the other materials he had collected, McCook decided that the wandering fraternity in the United States constituted a veritable army of approximately 50,000. The professor reminded his readers that there were fewer than that under Wellington's command at Waterloo. Later writers and sociologists placed the figure of road wanderers even higher. "So much driftwood," McCook lamented, "by what means and waves tossed, when and where to be finally engulfed!"

In lectures, speeches, and articles, McCook began to set forth various remedies for the plight of the shiftless sojourners. Liquor, he insisted, was perhaps the most ruinous evil. After several of his spying expeditions at local saloons, McCook determined that some of his boys were not uncommonly consuming upward of twenty-five drinks—more than four pints of whiskey—in twenty-four-hour periods. When

McCook asked the master of the Hartford almshouse for a list of inmates who hit the bottle excessively, the frustrated director threw up his hands. It would be far easier, he told the investigator, to draw up a list of the very few who did not. A Hartford politician who had once been Overseer of the Poor told McCook that 90 percent of the paupers were alcoholics. So interested did the professor become in this subject that he gathered together samples of whiskey from the skid road areas of Hartford and, with the help of a chemist at Trinity College, ran tests of the brews to determine whether the cheap brands swilled by the poor were more poisonous than higher-priced labels. To McCook's surprise, the analyses showed that the cheaper grades of liquor were actually less dangerous than the more expensive because they were watered down. The tests thus explained how a man could drink four pints of whiskey in one day and continue to live.

"Two habits have chiefly to do with the conditions of vagabond existence," McCook wrote, "the habit of idleness and the habit of intemperance: to which perhaps a third might be added: the habit of physical uncleanness." Although the professor opposed prohibition because of the problem of enforcement, he did suggest governmental control over the manufacture and distribution of alcohol. He recommended uniform state laws to commit drunkards and vagrants to detention centers for forced abstinence and forced work; strict laws against train jumping to be rigidly enforced; and an end of personal gifts of money to beggars. "The person who will give any beggar a coin just because it seems too hard to refuse him, ought on similar grounds to give razors and guns to madmen and children." A quick stake, he said, only kept the saloon doors swinging. McCook thus saw the vagrancy problem as a moral problem rooted in personal licentiousness and degeneracy. Even though he recognized the correlation between national economic distress and the number of men on the road, McCook still regarded the problem as essentially one of moral decay.

The Reverend insisted that tramps must be made to work for their lodging. He campaigned for a state reformatory system geared to rehabilitate the vagabonds, but his efforts were drowned in political bickering and misunderstanding. He lamented that the roots of the homeless wayfarer problem were so deep that only a miraculous social transformation could provide the total answer. "Abolish industrial booms," he wrote, "financial crises, business slumps, hard times! Encourage marriage! How? Do you ask? Really I don't know!"

McCook also recognized the paradox that many men who had been introduced to the nomadic life for whatever reason actually preferred it. "Apparently when the charm is broken," McCook noted, "and one discovers that virtue can be disposed with and that contentment can be had some other way, there are a great many who resign domesticity permanently. Just as a horse is spoiled for the harness when he has once or twice successfully run away." Some men find, McCook concluded, that "living and labor are not interchangeable terms!" McCook often heard the men of the road talk of the siren's call of wanderlust, the setting free of the spirit. Connecticut Fatty once said that there were only two really happy men in the world—the millionaire and the bum.

A curious ambivalence characterized McCook's work on the tramp phenomenon. He found most of the wanderers he met personally agreeable and even charming. "Give the tramp a chance!" he once wrote, "I know him very well. I have generally found him a pleasant, approachable fellow and I should rather take my chances of reforming him, with purely civil and secular measures, than the ordinary felon."

But the Reverend assumed that the homeless population was less a victim of social conditions than of personal moral degeneracy; less a result of economic depression than of individual character weakness. His answer to the dilemma posed by this mass of disaffiliated individuals was thus a traditional one—repression. Take away the tramp's free transportation; get him off the bottle; lock him up in institutions that force restraint and discipline. Only then could the vagrant be molded into a productive worker and an acceptable member of society.

The thought was certainly not unique. Many others in this period—social welfare workers, sociologists, officers of correction institutions, reformers, and journalists—began to assess the origins, threats, and possible remedies to the pauper class in the United States. Like McCook, most demanded vigorous repressive measures. Scores of vitriolic articles and tracts in the learned journals and especially in the press castigated the evil specter of the homeless class which seemed to loom darkly over the American social fabric. It made little difference if some of the writers found the problem closely linked with changes in the industrial order; if they found that the new corps of laborers on the road was filling critical labor demands; if stock-market crashes and financial depressions increased the numbers of road nomads dramatically; if all of the floating population was not made up of petty thieves and alkis. The message of most of the observers of the tramp and hobo world was clear. The road people were tainted with psychological disease and moral depravity. They were labeled undersocialized, sociopathic, anomic, kin-isolated, socially undernourished, negative-ego-image oriented, and a host of other appellations.

Orlando Lewis, the widely respected sociologist of the Charity Society of New York, echoed many when he declared that homeless men were products of their own moral inadequacies. All the jobless, he insisted, could get work if they really wanted it. Unemployment was a problem of motivation and not of the waves of the country's economic waters.

Defying labels and simple explanations, the disaffiliated roaming class remained an enigma. Trying to solve the puzzles of the behavior of the masses of nomadic, homeless men became a great challenge. In almost every case, however, the investigators began with the assumption that the class was somehow despoiled, alien, dangerous. One psychologist posed the following loaded question to a variety of individuals: "What is the matter with these men?" The answers were predictable: from an employer—the men are lazy, the vagrancy laws weak, and the charity organizations ineffectual; from a charity worker—the men are defective morally and physically, with some inheriting their defects but most simply acquiring them through bad habits and immorality; from a preacher—the men have lost sight of God; from an educator—the men lack vocational training and other skills to make them effective workers; from a reformer—the hydra-headed monsters drink and prostitution have taken their toll. The men on the road, most everyone agreed, were abnormal and their abnormalities were rooted in failure of personality and motivation.

John McCook studied the tramp and hobo community with more dedication than any other sociological investigator in the nineteenth century. He accumulated an unprecedented wealth of data on the subject. As he trailed the stiffs into bars in skid road districts of several cities, as he pored over the hundreds of questionnaires he received from many parts of the country, as he listened to the spiels of the grafters and hawkers, heard the tales of adventure and misery, saw the faces of the huddled forms on cheap lodging-house floors, as he learned the language and studied the habits of the men of the road, McCook found himself absorbed in a world unlike anything he had before known. He showed a measure of respect for the intelligence of the drifters, their ingenuity, wit, and courage; he sympathized with their pain. But the answer was still the same. Industrial causes, he finally concluded, had little to do with pauperism and vagabondage. The problem was with the men themselves. Along with most of the other writers of his day, he called for reformation—a crusade against liquor, begging, indolence, train jumping, and moral and physical filth.

John McCook never published the book on tramps he had planned. But the professor left a remarkable series of essays on tramp life and a body of information on the underclasses unparalleled in his day. He also left an admonition—a warning to all those who could fall under the bewitching spell of the road, to all who might forsake the order and discipline of the world to which the professor was himself wedded. But McCook's admonition, in its wistful description of the magnetism and seductive call of the wanderlust, betrayed a vicarious fascination with the world he could never personally know. "The average man grows up to live a regular life and to work as a part of it," he wrote. "We are taught to believe that there is a necessary relation between doing our daily tasks, eating our regular meals, going to bed in a fixed place, rising at a pre-arranged hour, wearing a certain kind of clothes, that there is between all this and being 'good' an unalterable relationship: as also between being good and being happy. Religion gives its awful sanction to this theory, habit fortifies it; successive generations of what we call civilization even create an instinct which even makes us think, or at least say, we like it: When suddenly to one of us comes the discovery that we can stop all this and yet live—nay, grow fat, perhaps, and vigorous and strong; drop worry and responsibility . . . go everywhere, see everything . . . and when that discovery comes, it is apt to be fatal."

4/ *Jockers, Moochers, and Thieves*

> *In the Big Rock Candy Mountains*
> *You never change your socks,*
> *And little streams of alcohol*
> *Come a-trickling down the rocks.*
> *The box cars are all empty*
> *And the railroad bulls are blind,*
> *There's a lake of stew and whiskey, too,*
> *You can paddle all around 'em in a big canoe*
> *In the Big Rock Candy Mountains.*

THE WELL-KNOWN folk song is a tramp's fantasy, the spiel of a seasoned jocker luring others into his world, a world of professed idleness, worship of the beauties of nature, and freedom and independence. It was, instead, a world where men conned and mooched for survival; slumped in boxcar corners, back alleys, and mission-house floors; and scratched calendars on jail-cell walls. This was the myth of the Big Rock Candy Mountains and reality of the tramp road. Jack London, who had traveled in this world, once called the tramps the "far-wanderers of Hoboland"—the con artists, grafters, panhandlers, shysters, and thieves of the tracks and the main stems. But if the tramps were "the far-wanderers," there were others on the road who moved in even more unconventional circles. These were the yeggs—hard-bitten, violent criminals and highwaymen of the freights. The world of the tramps and yeggs was a world of club and iron. It was a world in which the American hobo moved and with which he had to deal.

TRAMPS

RECOLLECTION (A BALLADE OF FORMER TRAMP DAYS)

The cars lay on a siding through the night;
The scattered yard lamps winked in green and red;
I slept upon bare boards with small delight,—
My pillow, my two shoes beneath my head;
As hard as my own conscience was my bed;
I lay and listened to my own blood flow;
Outside, I heard the thunder come and go
And glimpsed the golden squares of passing trains,
Or felt the cumbrous freight train rumbling slow;
And yet that life was sweet for all its pains.

Against the tramp the laws are always right,
So often in a cell I broke my bread
Where bar on bar went black across my sight;
On country road or rockpile ill I sped
Leg-chained to leg like man to woman wed,
My wage for daily toil an oath, a blow;
I cursed my days that they were ordered so;
I damned my vagrant heart and dreaming brains
That thrust me down among the mean and low—
And yet that life was sweet for all its pains.

I crept with lice that stayed and stayed for spite;
I froze in "jungles" more than can be said;
Dogs tore my clothes, and in a woeful plight
At many a back door for my food I pled
Until I wished to God that I was dead . . .
My shoes broke through and showed an outburst toe;
On every side the world was all my foe,
Threatening me with jibe and jeer and chains,
Hard benches, cells, and woe on endless woe—
And yet that life was sweet for all its pains.

The author was Harry Kemp, the tramp poet. "Freedom
is the one God I worship," he once told an interviewer. At
age twelve he left school to work at a celluloid factory. At
sixteen he jumped a German cattle ship bound for Australia.

He later turned up in China in time for the Boxer Rebellion. When he returned to America, it was as a poet, beating his way across the country with a volume of Christina Rossetti in his hip pocket, jotting down verse in a small notebook. He composed rhymes about hooking freights, loneliness, old stiffs he had seen on the road, and the exhilaration of moving. From inside jails he collected ballads and verse from his cellmates—prison songs, cocaine songs:

> *Oh, coco-Marie, and coco-Marai,*
> *I'se gon'ta whiff cocaine 'twill I die.*
> *Ho! (sniff) Ho! (sniff) baby, take a whiff of me!*

He copied them on pieces of wrapping paper that covered his food basket. The following song about the convict's most formidable enemy came from Kemp's time in a Texas jail:

> *There's a lice in jail*
> *As big as a rail;*
> *When you lie down*
> *They'll tickle your tail—*
> *Hard times in jail, poor boy!*

Diminutive and sickly as a child, Kemp worked all his life building his body and pushing himself to extraordinary physical limits. He became a bohemian of the tracks—food faddist, sometime nudist colony resident, ofttimes philanderer. It was Kemp, perhaps more than any other writer, who put into words the tramp worship of independence. Kemp once said that his greatest pleasure was "to vanish like smoke . . . to shout and sing for the sheer happiness of freedom from responsibility and regular work."

Whatever the individual causes of disaffiliation of the men of the road, and there were many—from bitterness over past jobs and periods of unemployment, to alcoholism, to personal or family tragedy—many found relief from the frustrations of traditional American society by adopting a new one, the tramp society, with new rules and new challenges. To survive, indeed to thrive, without work of any kind, to roam at will with only wit and guile as weapons—this was the spirit of the tramp community. Unlike the hobo who often prided himself on his work skills and his ability to take on different kinds of jobs under almost impossible conditions, the tramp, as Harry Kemp wrote, made aversion to work a profession. Consummate idlers, the tramps cultivated a science of survival. Begging, petty larceny, con jobs—the tramp practiced them all. If he practiced them well he made out. If he didn't, he died.

Jack London wrote of being drawn into the tramp world in the 1890s: "They were road kinds, and with every word they uttered the lure of The Road laid hold of me more imperiously. . . . And it all spelled Adventure: Very well; I would tackle this new world." London later called his new world "the pit, the abyss, the human cesspool, the shambles and charnelhouse of our civilization."

London's various essays on the world of the tramp detailed the personal odyssey of an eighteen-year-old "blond-beastly" Nietzschean into the world of the "submerged tenth," the sociologists' designation for the mysterious underclasses—the social pit, the sordid human cellar where, as London pointed out, men wage war among themselves over society's crumbs, where habitual discouragement and defeat bring a life of social debasement for some, a life of crime for others, and early death for many.

For Jack London, however, the tramp society held out the chance for aristocracy. He was young, tough, and intelligent. He quickly became a "profesh," a patrician of the order, the fittest survivor of jungle wars, maker and enforcer of law, the elite in a macho world of power in which squeamish weaklings were trampled. And London, as he so often reminded his readers, was not a squeamish weakling. He was among the swiftest, strongest, most clever, a profesh in every manner, giving lessons to gay cat amateurs and stew bums.

London did not remain on the road long. He had risen to the top of this world and others called. But even though disillusioned with its sordidness and depravity, he, like Harry Kemp, had felt the excitement of the road that compelled many young men of the late nineteenth century to join the tramp fraternity. He had mooched and conned and fought and had survived. "I lay on my back with a newspaper under my head for a pillow," he wrote. "Above me the stars were winking and wheeling in squadrons back and forth as the train rounded the curves, and watching them I fell asleep. The day was done—one day of all my days. Tomorrow would be another day, and I was young."

Like Harry Kemp and Jack London, O. Henry wrote of the tramp ideal of freedom. Whistling Dick, the tramp hero of an 1899 O. Henry short story, is offered a position of responsibility at a sugar plantation called Bellemeade as a reward for a good deed. After spending Christmas Eve in a quaint, spotless plantation bedroom, he goes to the window on Christmas morning to welcome in the fresh breezes; instead, he hears the dread sounds of an ancient enemy—work. "Already from the bosom of the mill came the thunder of rolling barrels of sugar, and (prison-like sounds) there was a great rattling of chains as the mules were harried with stimulant imprecations to their places by the wagon-tongues . . . and a toiling, hurrying, hallooing stream of workers were dimly seen in the half darkness loading the train with the weekly output of sugar. Here was a poem, an epic—nay, a tragedy—with work, the curse of the world, for its theme." The tramp clambers catlike out of a room he now sees as a prison, away from the chance for a "position," and into the welcome woods. Suddenly a birdlike, jubilant whistle is heard in the woods, a call of unbridled liberty.

The tramp's longing for and worship of the freedoms and bounties of nature are wonderfully illustrated by an idealized article entitled "The Jungle—An Idyl of the Springtime," which appeared around the turn of the century:

> You have been cooped up in the city all winter, sleeping in crowded fetid lodging houses, eating "coffee and's" or those mysterious compounds of the cheap restaurants called "stews." As you shuffle down the main stem some bright glorious spring morning you are conscious of a new wine-like fragrance in the air. There are no trees or grass in the city, but you know instinctively that somewhere, away from the bricks and mortar and crowds and "bulls," the golden spring sunshine is filtering down through the tender green leaves. You have a sudden and severe attack of the "wanderlust," your feet itch for strange ties, and before you realize the fact you are headed for the nearest freight yards. . . . Two days later you have found it. A little spot on the banks of a turbulent, brawling mountain brook, and basked by a semi-circle of trees, enveloped in a sort of mist of pale green. You have disposed of a hearty breakfast of ham, eggs, fried spuds and Java, all cooked in those handy utensils so thoughtfully provided by the Standard Oil Co. A good jungle stiff can make anything from a frying pan to bath tub out of them. You seek a grassy spot and lie down on the fragrant earth, the sunlight flecks the ground with little spots of pale gold. . . . You roll over on your back and watch the woolly little white clouds drifting across the blue sky and you don't know where you are going to go next or when or why nor where you are going to sleep tonight and don't care a damn either.

Thousands of families lost young sons, some barely out of knickers, to the road in the latter part of the century, many lured by tales spun by tramp jockers. The railroad yards were fertile recruiting grounds where wide-eyed boys wandered around water tanks and roundhouses and by the massive freights and dreamed of adventure that lay down the tracks. Yorkey Ned, a veteran tramp in the early 1900s, recalled hearing this song intoned around numerous jungle fires:

WHERE IS MY WANDERING BRAT TONIGHT?

Where is my wandering boy tonight?
The boy of his mother's pride,
Oh he's counting the ties with a bed on his back,
Or else he is dinging a ride.
Oh where is my boy tonight?
Oh where is my boy tonight?
He's on the head end of a cattle train, lady,
That's where y're brat is tonight.

His heart may be as pure as the morning dew,
But his togs are a sight to see,
If he's nailed for a vag, his plea won't do,
"Sixty days," said the judge, "you see."
Oh where is my boy tonight?
Oh where is my boy tonight?
The chilly wind blows, to the hoosegow he goes
That's where you're brat is tonight, lady.

I was lookin' for work, oh judge, he said.
Said the judge, "I've heard that crack before."
So to the tough chain gang he's led
To hammer the rocks some more.
Oh where is my boy tonight?
Oh where is my boy tonight?
To strike many blows for the country he goes,
That's where you're brat is tonight, lady.

Don't frisk for your wandering brat tonight,
Let him play the old game if he will
Let him carry his load to the end of the road,
For he can never be still.
Oh where is my boy tonight?
Oh where is my boy tonight?
Whereever he blows up against it he goes
Here's luck to your boy tonight, lady.

But not only young boys saw the promise of liberation and adventure in a life free from work and the stifling constraints of organized society. To some men, frustrated and embittered by loss of work or by unbearable work conditions, the tramp life offered an alternative. A jungle and boxcar could look good to a man made wretched by the numbing monotony of a factory or a murky coal-mine tomb.

Many in the tramp fraternity, however, were men who would have been virtually unemployable even if they had wanted jobs. One tramp remembered the words of a road comrade: "Liquor has made a goddam monkey outa me, Blondey. Sometimes I gits on the water wagon an' holes on tight. . . . But one drink! an' my God! I let go de rope wid bot' han's. I fall in de gutter on my royal American sitdownski. An' stay in a gutter until some bull comes along an' plays a tune on my soles nex' morning." Or as an old tramp verse lamented:

> *A woman frail*
> *And a glass o' ale*
> *Made a horse's tail*
> *Of me.*

Many men who joined the tramp ranks were ex-hoboes. The succession of hard, low-paying jobs persuaded many migrant laborers that work was, as the tramp fraternity had said all along, the scourge of mankind. And if he survived on the road without work for a period of time, the tramp initiate gained confidence. Jack London wrote, "From the knowledge that he has idled and is still alive, [he] achieves a new outlook on life . . . finally he flings his challenge in the face of society, imposes a valorous boycott on all work."

For many men on the road the caste distinctions between tramp and hobo meant little. They worked for periods of time, then led tramplike lives, and then took jobs once again. Others followed the caste lines more closely. Although tramps and hoboes often mixed in hobo jungles, on the freights, and on the city stems, the two classes generally had little respect for each other. The tramp usually considered the hobo a weakling who had resorted to demeaning jobs to survive, a sniveling patsy to society's norms. The hobo generally considered the tramp a worthless parasite.

It was around their own jungle campfires, away from the hobo, that the tramps found a sense of fraternity and identification. They sang. They told jokes and stories and composed rhymes. They fought. They conducted kangaroo courts, mock judicial proceedings before which one tramp after another was baited and sentenced. The punishment for one indiscreet insult might be a whipping and pounding by several other tramp brothers.

Godfrey Irwin, a longtime man of the road who was later recognized as an authority on tramp and hobo vernacular, remembered one evening beside a western railroad yard listening to the crackling of ties in the fire and the talk of tramps encircling the mulligan. An old sea stiff quietly recited several verses of John Masefield's "Sea Fever"; several tales about rattlesnakes and other poisonous reptiles led to the poem "The Gila Monster Route." From poetry to sex jokes to railroad ditties the conversation ranged. Irwin recalled many such nights—hard-bitten road stiffs quoting Kipling and Edgar Guest and Robert Service, songs and poems "on the rights of man and the confusion of the ruling class," to quote one of Irwin's road acquaintances. Even Jack London had been awed by tramps arguing philosophy and economic theory, by their erudition and forensic skills on a variety of subjects. After he heard a number of spirited arguments, London, still a teenager, decided he needed to read more widely. He later enrolled in an Oakland, California, high school.

There was little lovesick sentimentalism around the jungle fires but some ribald humor, much social parody, and ballads on the hard life of the road. There was much braggadocio of men recounting heroic journeys. Many of the stories in the jungles were designed to illustrate fine points of etiquette or moral lessons in the group's credo. The story of "Spider Kid" instructed the fraternity on the grim consequences for a boy who attempted to move from one jocker to another. Spider, it seems, dispatched his own jocker to the great boxcar in the sky because the jocker thwarted the boy's plan to join another tramp. The kangaroo court sentenced the wayward youth to the ultimate punishment—"greasing the track," death under the wheels of a freight train. The offending jocker, who had lured the boy from his master, got off somewhat more easily. He was knifed, kicked, and beaten senseless and barely escaped with his life.

The average tramp's arsenal of stories, even though embellished, was usually grounded in experience. His wanderings brought him into contact with many people and towns. As Jack London and other contemporary writers on the tramp psyche often remarked, one day in the life of a tramp was often filled with more memorable and often perilous occasions than a month or even a year would offer an American in a traditional job—from corporation executive to assembly-line laborer.

One of the favorite stories told over and over again in jungle camps involved a midnight raiding party of tramps in San Bernardino, California, and its prey—crates of chickens on a sidetrack by a railroad depot. Using a diversionary tactic, a burning freight car, the squad of tramps invaded the boxcar sanctuary of a large stock of Plymouth Rocks, Leghorns, and Rhode Island Reds and hauled the crates off to the tramp haven for sacrificial rites and a big feed. Other prowling parties brought back cabbage, potatoes, onions, and all the other necessary ingredients for a first-class feast. For three days, tramps for miles around shared in the bountiful mulligan. But there was more to the story. It seems that the stewed fowl were pedigreed birds, the products of scientific breeding, which were awaiting exhibition at a county fair. By the time railroad bulls began to scour the countryside, the perpetrators had vanished and left little trace. The theft went down in tramp lore as "The Million Dollar Mulligan."

Tramps also held conventions—not like the publicly advertised gatherings put on for hoboes, such as the annual bash at Britt, Iowa, but more secret affairs advertised by word of mouth through the tramp world. Some of the conventions were held almost annually, with tramps arriving on the rods and gunnels from all parts of the country. Around the turn of the century, tramps gathered for several conventions in Green Island, Iowa, a small town on the Mississippi River where two railroad lines crossed. On one occasion, several participants reported that seventeen wagonloads of beer were swilled in one day. Jockers and punks, cripples and paralytics, the profesh and the initiates—they all came to drink and sing, to argue, and to feast on vats of mulligan. Inevitably during a convention one bard would compose a song which memorialized the event and included in the lyrics the principal tramp figures. "At Fresno" tells of a tramp convention held in the late nineteenth century:

> *... Some came from the old Buckeye State,*
> *Some came from Boston, Mass.*
> *That afternoon the tenth of June*
> *They gathered there en masse.*
> *From the Lone Star State came Dallas Jim*
> *And Red the Katydid,*
> *From Kalamazoo with Dirty Lew*
> *Came the Sacramento Kid.*
>
> *Ohio Dan and Frisco Red*
> *Blew in with Salina Jack,*
> *Irish Shang from the old Boo Gang*
> *And Big Mack from Hackensack.*

Often heard but seldom seen
Was the bum called Lousey Mike,
Jimmy the Sneak from Cripple Creek
And old St. Louis Pike.

K. C. Bill all dressed to kill
Shook hands with Boston Red,
While High Card Joe from Buffalo
Played cards with Portland Ned.
Louisville Slim and Portland Paul
Fixed up a jungle stew,
While Cockney Tim and Soft Collar Slim
Sneered gumps for our menu.

Seldom Seen spieled out a song
Along with old Chi Sam,
And the Salina Shark from Central Park
Clog danced with Frisco Dan.
So we gathered round the jungle smudge
The night was goin' fast
We'd all served time in every clime
And the guff was of the past.

Much of the talk in the jungles and conventions focused
on the central problem of the tramp existence—how to survive without work of any kind. Tramps swapped stories
about dangerous railroad lines and sadistic bulls, about
towns that would vag a stiff for little or no cause, about famous con jobs and effective rackets, and on methods of panhandling. Several enterprising tramps over the years even
drew up instructions for those engaged in the ancient art of
"throwing the feet." One such list of helpful hints for beggars included the following:

1) avoid the south; hitting up individual southerners for a
   meal is something that Mr. Ripley will be anxious to
   hear about; southern country hospitality to beggars
   consists of sending out a reception committee of
   hounds.
2) avoid foreigners and women; the former will think they

are being taken as usual and the latter will be insulted
if approached on the streets.

3) pick laborers or shabby looking men; the less wealthy
prefer to believe that they belong to a class that gives
rather than a class that receives.

4) never whine or weep; pretend that you are of the same
ilk as the guy you are hitting up and he will likely sym-
pathize with your current predicament.

5) prostitutes, as a class, are the most generous; feeling
morally superior only to moral men and married
women, prostitutes like to atone for their sins with acts
of generosity; they are also, contrary to popular belief,
somewhat sentimental.

6) avoid Protestant clergymen; they will raise your hopes,
waste your time, and send you along with nothing
more than pompous commandments.

7) Catholic sisters are good marks; all of them are, if sometimes gloomy, at least good-natured toward the needy.

One favorite jungle story about an inspired racket and the
tramp that pulled it off involved a stiff named Jerry McCau-
ley. Jerry used the "Sallys," the Salvation Army stations, as
his places of business. He would march into a Sally with
several young punks in tow and offer them on the gospel
bench as converts to the Lord. Jerry carefully instructed or
threatened his charges to sit for hours before the preacher's
drone. For this, they received bed and supper and Jerry received a reward for his missionary activity—a pair of shoes,
a worn overcoat, or some groceries. The business thrived so
well that Jerry accumulated an impressive stock of used
clothing which he stashed in a tin-sheeted hut, a stock that
he bartered for pints of rotgut, sweepstakes tickets, and an
occasional use of other stiffs' women friends. When business
was slow, Jerry would head for the pawnshops. Jerry kept at
the racket for nearly twenty years until he nearly died one
winter night in 1919 in a Michigan jail cell with double
pneumonia brought on by a protracted affair with the bottle

and overexposure. Tramps for years afterward told how Jerry actually got religion scared into him during those nights, how the shyster con artist would throw himself on the jail floor wailing in earnest the prayers he had heard for years in the Sally services. Jerry finally quit the tramp life, settled in New York's Bowery, and set up a mission of his own. Tramps remembered seeing Jerry on early morning begging excursions knocking on doors in all kinds of weather, not for himself but for his mission. He fed starving men in his soup kitchen and gave away items of clothing. One of his friends wrote, "Somehow the Blood of the Lamb must have seeped into his veins during all those years of out-smarting the gospel mongers."

Jerry's end was not typical. Stories are legion about tramps spending their final hours crumpled in lonely boxcar corners; of men coughing and spitting their last consumptive days on floors of nickel flophouses; of others hacked to death in private wars with other tramps or wiped out by bulls and dicks; of train jumpers mangled beneath freight-car blades; of stiffs frozen to death in city gutters.

As was the case with their road counterparts, the hoboes, the greatest challenge for the tramps was to survive the dreaded winters. The usual winter havens for the men of the road were, of course, the main stems. But some guys hated the cities so much that they constructed winter hovels in which to shack up until spring. Usually slapped together with cardboard, tar paper, and whatever lumber was avail-able, the huts were airy and cold but, to those who took the time to build them, preferable to a grungy, rat-infested mis-sion or lodging house. To the guys attempting to maintain such quarters, a winter stake was imperative for food and other supplies. If a tramp had not been particularly suc-cessful panhandling in earlier months or if he had been rolled toward the end of the summer, he would most likely have to head for a city whether he liked it or not.

Because of their unbending antipathy to work, the tramps had fewer options than hoboes on the stems. The hoboes, for example, could head for a wayfarers' lodge. The one in Baltimore accommodated 125 persons a night. It strictly enforced its consecutive three-day limit of shelter, its demand for wood sawing and splitting, its compulsory hot bath with carbolic soap, and its nightly disinfection of clothes—all under close supervision. Although some hoboes could endure this kind of regimentation and the work that went along with it, the tramps avoided such places. A tramp's aversion to work could be so great that he would walk himself tired looking for a handout rather than accept a job on the woodpile. Pride, reputation, honor—all would be lost. And to the tramps such self-respect, however battered by the realities of life on the road, was important.

Through their stories and songs, fraternal codes of behavior, monickers, and language, the tramps maintained this affected dignity. Even the comedians who parodied the tramp figure played on the image of his shabby nobility. When Charlie Chaplin, down to his last cent, chose to eat his shoes, he did it with flair, twirling the laces like spaghetti. Emmet Kelly, the clown who shuffled through the sawdust of thousands of circus rings playing a disheveled stiff, sported a clothespin tie clasp and puffed on a stogie.

As writers and sociologists tried to lift the shroud of mystery which surrounded the tramp community in the late 1800s, they were told by many in the fraternity that tramping was an honorable calling, that great men of the past, led by Christ himself, had carried the tramp banner proudly. Shakespeare, Ben Jonson, Oliver Goldsmith—each had at one time the requisite qualifications for the badge of trampdom—no money, influence, vote, or job. But they had wild liberty and buoyancy and from such stuff springs the genuis

of nations. Without men on the bum, tramps claimed, there
would be less art, less literature, less appreciation of nature.
The *National Labor Tribune* reported in December 1876
that "Christianity was ushered into existence by tramps. . . .
Great movements came from the bottom layer of society,
who possess the truest instincts and the noblest instincts."

But as much as tramps invoked the spirit of the open road
and the glory of nature, as much as they talked of freedom
from responsibility and work, their experience on the road
seemed to bely the posturing. Arthur Todd, a sociologist at
the University of Illinois, wrote in 1913 that the tramps'
praise of freedom and independence was so much bunk.
Maybe one in a hundred tramps, he charged, was the idealistic sojourner in search of ultimate truths, the dreamer living
in nature's garden; the others were parasites, antisocial misfits whose philosophy of life conformed to the American
proverb: "The world is a fat sheep's tail; man is the knife."

The sociologist was only echoing the opinions of the fore-
most writers on tramp life in the country—Josiah Flynt and
Jim Tully. Flynt had been raised in the house of his aunt
Frances E. Willard, the temperance leader. In obvious rebellion against his stuffy confines, Flynt made his life a succession of escapes. Ending his college days early by hopping
a freight, he landed in reform school for stealing a buggy.
Breaking out of this institution, just as he had broken out of
his home and school, he hit the rails, wandering in tramp society for eight months. In 1899 Flynt published *Tramping
with Tramps*, an amateurish but fascinating sociological investigation of the road. The book became the great encyclopedia for later writers on the tramp phenomenon. It out-
lined, as no work had done before, the haunts and habits of
this wandering band. If Walt Whitman had extolled the song
of the open road, Flynt attacked its discordant notes and
tried to rupture what he saw as the tramp myth. Sordid, de-

graded, debauched—life on the road, he wrote, did not bring
a freeing of the spirit; it brought disease, crime, and death.
Later rebelling once again against a former life, Flynt ironi-
cally became a railroad detective and crime reporter.

Jim Tully, born into oppressive poverty in an Ohio shan-
tytown, traveled various roads—tramping, circus life, professional boxing, and Hollywood. He wrote of them all in a
kind of brawny, brawling prose. In 1924 he published *Beggars of Life*, a brooding panorama of the dark side of
American life. He dedicated the book to his friend Charlie
Chaplin, for whom he had worked as a ghost writer. Like
Josiah Flynt, Jim Tully had personally tasted the strains and
beatings of the road; seen men killed, maimed, and emotionally destroyed; shared mulligan and jail cells; sung tramp
songs and grubbed for pennies and food. He had watched
"floppers" squatting on sidewalks with pleading hands
upraised; seen "halfies," train jumpers who had lost both
legs above the knee, hobble around jungle camps; and had
grown used to the sight of dazed, rummy stiffs stumbling
along back alleys. This was not the Big Rock Candy Mountains, the land of lemonade springs and lakes of stew.

In one of Jim Tully's short stories, several weatherbeaten
vagabonds are talking about the oppressive heat. A lone-
legged stiff remarks that the boys are getting punished for
their sins. " 'It'll be hotter'n this when you git punished for
your sins, One Leg,' grunted a heavy man with a red ker-
chief around his neck. 'Maybe so, maybe so,' drawled One
Leg. 'I been punished enough in my time for all I ever
done.' "

YEGGS

> *As the gondola rolled onward*
> *The boy stood on the deck,*

Thinking of those happy days
Before he met "John Yegg."

A mendicancy officer of the New York Charity Organization Society told of hearing this refrain and other similar
doggerel in county jails, city workhouses, and other correc-
tional institutions at the turn of the century. It was the lament of young recruits in the ranks of yeggdom, or "The
Johnson Family," as yeggs called themselves, the class of
tramps which made the road a criminal playground—from
blowing safes to robbing banks. If hoboes generally despised
most tramps, they considered yeggs especially loathsome.
Many a hobo lost his stake and sometimes his life at the
hands of these road thugs.

"Old Texas Dutch," a German-born burglar, was the legendary founder of the yegg order in the days just before the
Civil War. Dutch was credited with discovering the antidote
to a bloodhound on the hunt—oil of mustard. No bloodhound, the yeggs claimed, ever treed a stiff who used this
magic herb. But alas! Old Dutch, as the story goes, forgot his
oil of mustard after a Georgia heist and a hound ran him
down and chewed him up. Dutch died in a hospital. But for
years afterward yeggs paid homage to their fallen martyr—
the best of the "Johns."

The world of yeggdom was a world of petermen, dips, and
fences. Around the campfires of this group the talk turned to
the art of cracking safes and casing banks. The language was
imaginative. An "obey" was a post office and "stickers" were
what the obies sold for mailing letters. A bank was a "jug."
A yegg used "grease" or "soup" (nitro) to blow obey and
jug "petes" (safes) and always kept "tin ears" for "night
hacks" who might be lurking about on guard. He used a
"screw" to open all manner of doors. The moon was the "old
stool pigeon" and when it shone brightly the Family lay
low. When the yegg moved on with his take, he hopped a

"John O'Brien" (boxcar). One writer who spent several months traveling with members of the Family remembered a typical line: "John, I catted around in the obie—old box, soft iron, no glim burning over it at night . . . I figure there's five in it."

Sometimes gangs of yeggs set up separate camps replete with tools of the trade; often they infested the hobo jungles for periods of time, then drifted on. At one yegg camp in 1915, detectives found an arsenal of 200 pounds of tools, 500 detonating caps, electric lead wires, assorted automatic revolvers, and cans of nitro. One police official in 1907 asked despairingly, "What can you do when the bank robber comes into town ragged and on foot . . . does his job, and steals a ride on a freight train to get away?" An old-time yegg named Yorkey Ned remembered this song from the turn of the century:

THE SAFECRACKER

Hi! That's what I am be God,
A knight of the puff and rod [powder and gun].
I'm an old time rock from the Q,
And with me brace to me shoulder,
I'm all the more bolder,
The Main Stem I prowl for a mark.
I've laid many of 'em low, Bo,
For I'm a knight of the old puff and rod.

To the discriminating yegg, the post offices were more inviting than the banks; at least the possible consequences of being caught were more inviting. As any veteran could testify, the federal pens meant lighter sentences, more commodious accommodations, and closer association with comrades. Leavenworth was regarded by many of the Johnson Family as a kind of vacation spot. On the other hand the state penitentiaries, yeggs complained, were manned by Bible-pounding wardens and staffed by bloodthirsty guards.

It was in the yegg community that the jocker-punk rela-
tionships were most intense and sometimes vicious. Like
men at sea, the hobo and tramp classes were largely womanless and homosexual behavior was not uncommon. Much of
it was anything but closeted. Around some jungle campfires
might be several tramps dubbed by their wolves as "Mabel"
or "Susan" or referred to as "my sweetie" or "the old lady"
or "Mother." The sociologist Nels Anderson remembered
"Mother Jones," a well-dressed man, telling him, "I never
saw a boy I couldn't get next to." A tramp who traded harrowing days of hooking freights for hooking other tramps in
the cities, "Mother" spent his summer days in Chicago's
Grant Park and winters in hotel lobbies looking for conquests.

One tramp wrote of his first contact with a jocker: "In
Wenatchee, Washington, I saw for the first time what we
wanderers on the road call a 'wolf.' The polite term would
be pederast. He was a horrible-looking individual with red
hair, bent nose, and repulsive lips. . . . With the wolf was a
pretty-faced boy—he could not have been over twelve years
old. 'He's the best little bum y'ever saw,' said the wolf. 'See
this sack of sandwiches? He mouched it. We never goes hungry, does we, kid? He gets us money, clothes, food, yeah,
and even shoes. Don'cha kid?' The youngster responded
with a forced grin." One of the more famous tramp songs
tells the story of a kid and jocker:

> Oh, when I was a little boy
>   I started for the West,
> But I hadn't got no further than Cheyenne
>   When I met a husky "burly"
> Who was rather poorly dressed,
>   And he flagged me with a big lump and a can.
>
> When I saw that cup of coffee,
>   How it made me think of home!

"Won't you let me have some,"
　　Said I, "Good Mister Bum?"
　　　Remember you were once a kid yourself."

He looked at me quite fiercely
　　O'er his grizzled, gray mustache;
On his weather-beaten face appeared a frown.
　　He said, "You little bummer,
　　What for should you pling me?
　　　Why don't you batter privates up in town?"

He asked me what my age might be;
　　I told him just sixteen,
That Boston was the town that I came from.
　　In his eyes appeared a stare,
　　"I think you I will snare,
　　　For you surely have the makings of a bum."

There are many stories of boys kidnapped by force or lured into concubinage, induced to beg money, food, and clothes for their captors, and sexually molested. Not surprisingly, many of these kids were runaways from orphanages or had spent time in reformatories. In addition to begging responsibilities, boys were forced to become valets, ministering to the jocker's every need—shaving, washing clothes, sewing. In return for sexual favors and these other ministrations, the jockers taught their punks the ways of tramp life—from survival on the road to the con jobs to the more specialized arts such as blowing safes.

Many tramp jockers resorted to grisly measures to make their apprentices more salable on the begging market. The usual method was to burn the boy's arm with lye or cantharides, causing sores which the yeggs called "lye bugs." If the jocker sent the boy to a physician, the wound would often be diagnosed as lupus vulgaris or tuberculosis of the skin. Many doctors ("crokers") would gladly provide the lad with a letter explaining his condition and would assume that the boy would deliver it to the local relief officials

or others in a position to give help. The letter would instead
become a first-class mooching ticket. Any self-respecting citizen with an ounce of pity was sure to be touched by the pa-
thetic sight of a dirty, forlorn waif with an arm that looked
hideously diseased and a physician's letter as proof. But
begging was not the only mission of the yegg gunsel. As he
picked up cash, food, and clothing from sympathetic benefactors, the boy was playing scout, sizing up the town and its
safes, memorizing valuable information for his jocker back in
camp.

The punks served apprenticeships of several years. If they
survived and had not incurred the wrath of the fraternity,
they could look forward to certification as master cracksmen.
In the pens, where a lot of the young prushins ended up, the
boy faced a special period of initiation. If he moved well
among the yegg prison population and made close associations, if he stayed out of trouble and didn't succumb to the
efforts of prison officials to make him a stool, he could find
the pen a valuable training ground. The experience could be
his key to acceptance.

The yegg community could boast of many colorful figures, and none was more colorful than Eddie Fay, "Sacramento Eddie," safecracker and burglar extraordinaire. Frail,
professorial, Eddie was a man of prodigious energy and keen
intellect. He read Anatole France and Goethe, recited Swinburne and Shelley, and revered Wagner and Beethoven. De-
bussy he couldn't stomach. "That frog," Eddie complained,
"writes tubercular music. His Pelleas and Melisande sounds
like something that came out of a hop fiend's brain." After
thirty years of blowing safes, an inspired Eddie hit upon a
grand scheme—the organization of a national union of
cracksmen. He would enlist a cadre of scouts to case obies
and banks nationwide. He would compile a master file replete with information on habits of individual night watch-

men, amounts of money typically on hand, and escape routes. He would charge a healthy fee for union member-ship, but would arrange for legal defense in case of arrest and provide for escape in case of conviction. Eddie teamed up with one "Sheenie Si" in the scheme and this proved to be his downfall. After a personal quarrel, Sheenie, who was to be the business manager of the cracksmen brotherhood, croaked Eddie in a South Side alley of Chicago. With Eddie's demise came the end of the union. But it brought the beginning of a yegg legend.

If Eddie Fay had been more cerebral in his approach to the yegg vocations of blowing obie safes and robbing banks, Jimmie McDougall played a more traditional role. Jimmie led a pack of yegg marauders which terrorized upper New York State in the early 1900s. When police finally netted Jimmie McDougall in Rochester in 1902, they were in for a surprise. Jimmie was actually Theresa McDougall, a former actress from Cleveland. Dressed in shoes several sizes too big, blue overalls, and a large flannel shirt, Theresa or "Jim-mie" had hoodwinked her yegg traveling companions for several years. She had been lucky that the tramps under her command hadn't discovered her secret. She would likely have suffered swift retribution from men with severely wounded pride.

Two areas of the country were hit particularly hard by roving yegg gangs carrying guns, knives, razors, coupling pins, and other weapons. The Blue Mountain "hump" in Oregon became notorious territory for yegg highwaymen, and many hoboes returning from lumber camps and can-neries with a winter stake were rolled and often killed. The most infamous gang in the United States was "The Lake Shore Push," which operated out of Cleveland. William Aspinwall, the hobo correspondent of sociologist John J. McCook, wrote of the Lake Shore gang: "They do not hesitate as I am told by Hobos to commit any kind of crime. They Rob and even murder Hobos that do not belong to their Gang. I was told a young boy probably 16 or 18 y old from Kalamazoo, Mich hapened to jump into a box car to beat his way and there was a number of the above Gang in the Car. They striped the young fellow of everything but his Pants & Shirt, Committed sodomy on his person and then threw the fellow out while the train was running at full speed. The fellow was found with his shoulder broke and otherwise cut and bruised up more dead than alive."

In the jungles and on the freights, the American hobo, "the working class of the road," encountered an assortment of stickup men and thieves all eager to "harvest the harvester." The hobo shared the road reluctantly with con men, safe blowers, burglars, and murderers on the run, seeking anonymity and sanctuary. The hobo often felt the whip of frustrated arms of the law which considered all men of the road criminal parasites and yegg marauders. The class distinctions of the vagabond community meant little to harassed sheriffs and railroad dicks facing repeated attacks by such groups as the Lake Shore Push. When increasing acts of vandalism by the road bums sparked increased efforts to rid the countryside of the nuisance, hobo heads were broken along with those of the tramps and yeggs.

"The pit, the abyss, the human cesspool," Jack London had called the tramp life. If the poet Harry Kemp remembered the life as "sweet for all its pains," he had an option to get out of it, an option he exercised. For many on the run— alcoholics, criminals, young boys from broken or poverty-wracked homes, the disillusioned and despairing, the men who no longer found identification with a society that had ground them down—there seemed to be no other options. They just kept looking for the ultimate con and the lakes of stew and whiskey.

In the Big Rock Candy Mountains
The jails are made of tin,
And you can bust right out again
As soon as they put you in;
The farmer's trees are full of fruit,
The barns are full of hay,
I'm going to stay where you sleep all day,
Where they boiled in oil the inventor of toil,
In the Big Rock Candy Mountains.

5/ "Not a Bum"

IN MAY 1893 William Aspinwall, "Roving Bill," the itinerant mushfaker who corresponded with sociologist John J. McCook, wrote, "Now I want you to distinctly understand me. I am not a Bum. I'd rather be kicked than go up to a House and ask for something to eat. I have went hungry many a time almost starve before I would ask. I often wished I was more of a Bum when I was good and hungry."

In 1917 an article in a railroad magazine declared, "It is through our easy methods that the roving gangs of hoboes and criminals, authors of some of the worst depravity and of some of the most hideous crimes, not to mention a regime of thievery and spoliation, are encouraged year after year to crawl under the social surface." The "hoboes and criminals," the article charged, were responsible not only for robbery, assault, and other crimes but for spreading immorality and laziness and setting an example of pauperism which was unhealthy for American society. In *A Son of the Middle Border*, Hamlin Garland wrote of tramping along the Connecticut River with a friend looking for work and getting only contemptuous stares from suspicious farmers. Broke and tired, the two men slept in oat shocks and graneries. "Each day the world grew blacker," Garland recalled, "and the men of the Connecticut Valley more cruel and relentless." The two began to understand the frustration of other roving vagabonds in search of work and a modicum of comfort on the road. "To plod on and on into the dusk, rejected of comfortable folk, to couch at last with pole-cats in a shock of grain is a liberal education in sociology."

The anger and bitterness of Connecticut Valley farmers,

railroad employees, and others who had suffered injury at the hands of criminal road thugs is understandable. And it is also understandable that this animosity and hostility were directed at hobo itinerant workers as well as burglars and highwaymen. To those outside the army of road wanderers, the men appeared very much alike. Most of those on the road, whether hobo or yegg, wore shabby clothes and flipped freights, panhandled and jungled, and dropped their real names for monickers. They mingled on the main stems of cities in winters, queued up in soup lines, and slept on cheap lodging-house floors. Almost all of them had seen the inside of "boodle" jails and had done time on rock piles. To the farmer who had seen gangs of brutal yeggs terrorizing the countryside or to a railroad shack who had seen a buddy knifed and thrown to the cinders, the army of road wanderers seemed to be a homogeneous group, alien and despicable, a menace and threat to society.

To the roving stiff looking for a job, the unfavorable public image—the linking of the hobo with the tramp—was not only demoralizing but many times self-fulfilling. One worker of the road, after nights on mission floors and in haystacks, after the soup lines and the lice and insults, wrote, "I have lost my loyalties to my country, to God, to mankind; that I have lived like an animal, I am taking on the ethics of an animal; that I have become, in short, a public menace."

But the image of the American man of the road had another side from that of public menace. If the hobo/tramp seemed a genuine threat to American society, his caricature could provoke laughter. From cartoonist Frederick Opper who originated "Happy Hooligan" to A. B. Frost and Nat Wills on stage, the road wanderer became a wistful comic character. In Charlie Chaplin the image was fully developed—the "Little Tramp," pathetically dressed in floppy trousers and oversize shoes but with a jaunty bearing,

trimmed mustache, cane, derby, and sprightly walk. "You
know, this fellow is many-sided," Chaplin once told Mack
Sennett, "a tramp, a gentleman, a poet, a dreamer, a lonely
fellow, always hopeful of romance and adventure."

In cartoons, articles, plays and motion pictures the image
emerged—the forlorn wayfarer in a losing war against life's
vicissitudes, the shaggy demeanor, the slapstick bouts with
railroad dicks and fierce dogs, the determination to plunge
ahead against all manner of slings and arrows lying in wait.
The figure was usually unshaven and crimson-nosed. He
sometimes carried from his shoulder a red-bandana bundle
tied to a stick. Yet Harry Kemp remarked that in all of his
pilgrimages on the road he had never seen a stiff carrying a
bundle wrapped in a bandana.

Famed circus clown Emmet Kelly once said that there
was much pathos connected with the hobo. "This explains
my success. People enjoy feeling sorry for the down-and-
outer who ceaselessly expends himself in an attempt to
accomplish something and never quite succeeds." But the
pathos was directed at a fabrication. The figure for whom
audiences had sympathy was not a recognizable human
being but a caricature well divorced from the real world. An
audience, even one which harbored fears of and disgust for
the actual thousands of men trudging along the tracks, could
feel themselves at a safe distance from real denizens of the
road and could thus find amusement in the ludicrous appearance of the comic tramp, the alien settings in which he found
himself, and his succession of futile battles. It was this in-
congruity—the image of the forlorn nomad confronting the
ordered, conventional, modern society—that newspapers
and the entertainment industry continued to cultivate and
exploit. When the hobo king and celebrity Jeff Davis signed
on to play a bit part in the movie *The Arkansas Traveler*,
his hosts in Hollywood persuaded him to pose on the floor

Free Lunch Room, Chicago, 1930

Wayfarer's Lodge, 5:45 A.M., Boston, Jan. 1895, Earning Breakfast

Wayfarer's Lodge, 6:45 A.M., Boston, Jan. 1895, Breakfast

The Bath, 11 P.M., Wayfarer's Lodge, Boston, January, 1895

Pitt and Green Street Mission, Boston, 1895

Seven-cent lodging house, East side New York, February 22, 1895

*Ben Reitman (center) and General Jacob Coxey (left)
at Chicago's Hobo College, 1928*

*Last of a Kind: Umbrella Mender (Mushfaker)
Near Brooklyn Bridge, January 11, 1950*

Sparky Smith

Frisco Jack

Steam Train Maury Graham

before a prop steak as if he were about to dig in, doggy-style.

While the comic image made the roving vagabond a less ominous and more humorous figure, it confirmed, at the same time, the widely held assumption that the shaggy pilgrim at the back door was a fairly worthless dolt. It would have been very difficult for any audience to imagine Charlie Chaplin or Emmet Kelly ever harvesting grain in the Dakotas or working the timberlands of the Northwest or the berry fields of California.

On the one hand the tramp/hobo figure was seen as a menace to society; on the other, as a dusty but good-natured clown. The American public thus remained oblivious to the reality of life on the road for the itinerant worker.

THE "MILLIONAIRE HOBO"

"Mission stiffs, panhandlers, bums and strike-breakers are not allowed here. Get out!" Dangling in the window of a first-floor room on Callowhill Street, Philadelphia, a small pasteboard sign greeted visitors. Other signs—"Join the union" and "Hobo Employment Bureau"—flanked it. In Philadelphia, as in numerous other large cities at the turn of the century, an organization known as the International Brotherhood Welfare Association set up an agency to assist "bona fide" hoboes in their endless quest for jobs and to provide them much-needed fellowship while they wintered on the main stems. The IBWA set out to destroy the notion that the hobo was picking the bones of American society while contributing nothing to it. The image of the hobo as a worthless and sometimes violent parasite was, the IBWA proclaimed, dead wrong.

Joe Millar, a calloused campaigner on the freights who claimed to have crossed the country a hundred times, explained to a reporter in Philadelphia the organization's exclusionary policies: "The hobo is the itinerant laborer, the fellow who saws lumber in Maine one week and punches cattle in Texas the next." Hoboes, Millar explained, worked for their lodging and meals on the road; bums and panhandlers, on the other hand, were only derelicts looking for a free ride, contemptible scum preying on and giving the hard-working stiffs of the road a bad name. The real hoboes, Millar insisted, despised the seedy vultures with their fast cons and rackets. To certify membership in the higher order, Millar and other full-fledged members of the hobo union carried cards bearing the IBWA insignia.

For the skinners and ice harvesters, the berry grabbers and oyster glommers, the apple knockers and spud diggers, for the hop pickers, all the migrant stiffs, the IBWA held out the vision, however ephemeral, of shorter work days, free transportation to and from job sites, abolition of the nefarious private employment agencies, free municipal baths and laundries, and unemployment insurance so that, as one hobo remarked, "the fellows can eat without panhandlin' when they can't get a job." But more than the promise of fighting for traditional labor demands, the IBWA pledged to educate the typical road worker, raise his intellectual sights, and prepare him to confront the hostile society crushing him underfoot.

By 1919 the organization, headquartered in Cincinnati, could boast of locals in fifteen cities. To the men of the road they became known as "Hobo Colleges." Night after night a few ill-clad, grizzled veterans of the tracks gathered in rented skid-road locations to hear lecturers expound on such esoteric subjects as the wage system of the Hungarian Republic and man's relation to the cosmic infinite and to such practical matters as vagrancy laws and venereal disease.

The IBWA and its colleges were the brainchild of a tall, gaunt, bearded socialist named James Eads How. More than any benefactor before or after, How poured heart, soul, and fortune into uplifting the masses of American hoboes. "The laboring man," he once declared at a college gathering, "has listened and clapped and cheered the sentiments of people he can not understand. He has done all this too long. Now the time has come when he is going to learn about society, and all the rest of it for himself." How saw the colleges as oases in which road stiffs could feel safe and welcome. "If he is penniless," How promised, "we sustain him. He always repays the kindness when he finds work. We try to show him that he will play an important part in the coming change and that he must take an interest in the study of industry and social and economic conditions. Needless to say, the kind of education we want him to get is not the kind the Chambers of Commerce or the Bankers' Associations are interested in."

James Eads How's paternal grandfather, John How, was mayor of St. Louis several times before the Civil War; his father, James F. How, was vice-president and general manager of the Wabash railroad; his maternal grandfather, James Buchanan Eads, was the builder of the Eads Bridge across the Mississippi River at St. Louis. Educated at Harvard, Meadville Theological Seminary, and the College of Physicians in St. Louis, How became a licensed physician but, much to the chagrin of his family, never a practicing one. Instead, rebelling against his patrician upbringing, How began to live a spartan life-style. He furnished his home with only the barest necessities, wore threadbare clothes, and adopted a scanty vegetarian diet. He often fasted. After his father died in St. Louis, How received $20,000 and gave it to the mayor with vague instructions to return it to the people who had earned it—the poor. When his mother died, he inherited approximately $200,000 and received other monies from tolls paid at the Eads Bridge. Not surprisingly, How, considered a hopeless and embarrassing eccentric by most of his family, found some of the inheritance tied up in a legal imbroglio. He nevertheless had a considerable fortune to spend and with it he began his crusade for social justice.

How first attempted to organize a nonsectarian monastic order called the Brotherhood of the Daily Life. He later worked as a laborer and preached social gospel during lunch hours. But his great effort was the IBWA, through which he sought to establish social bonds and solidarity for the homeless. He described the hobo colleges as "the migratory workers' university" where men of the road could be exposed to theories of labor, economics, political systems, and industrial law. When asked whether the intellectual fare served up at the meetings was a bit too deep for the dusty travelers of the road, How would bristle. If a hobo knew industrial law, for example, he would be better equipped to fight for his rights in the courts. "You know," How remarked, "people laugh at the idea of hoboes getting together to talk politics and labor problems. They think statesmen should have a monopoly in the discussion of these affairs. . . . The hobo has every right that patriotic people are bound to respect. The hobo laborer is doing fundamental work. It is the business of society to recognize this fact. And, remember, a hobo is not ashamed to be a hobo. He is a worker who lives on the sweat of his face."

Many hoboes were avid readers of newspapers and had strong opinions on the nation's affairs. From park benches to jungle fires, hoboes debated with conviction, and sometimes aggression, everything from free silver to the open door. They eagerly listened to impassioned soapboxers and curbstone orators talk of the single tax. They heard lecturers preach on anarchism and socialism. Some hoboes became champions of Henry George; others, of William Jennings Bryan. Most vented their ire at trusts and syndicates and the viper capitalists, Ford and Rockefeller. Through the college forums, How tried to stimulate and channel the intellectual energy he found among the hobo workers.

Interviewed in New York by a *Tribune* reporter in 1919 shortly after opening a college at 202 Bowery, How remarked, "At 9:30 in the morning the students assemble to see if there are any prospects of a job in sight. Should they fail in getting a job we meet at 11:30 and try to find out why there are so many more men than there are jobs. We study civil economics for an hour. Then we join in a light luncheon, and after that we study industrial law."

Heavily tinctured with the socialist message, the curriculum also included instruction in health and nutrition. But the principal mission was to add meditative light to dreary lives. To reporters or other outside observers walking in on such meetings, the sight of bedraggled figures listening to a spirited discourse on the work of the Liberal Socialist League must have seemed more than slightly comic. But How, somehow dignified and stately in his own baggy clothes, was intensely serious. He traveled the country giving lectures on labor problems and socialist theory. He invited an array of speakers to hobo college meetings. He began to hold conventions where the same kind of fare was served up—talks on abstract economic theories and political philosophy. The conventions normally adopted formal resolutions and drew up petitions to Congress pleading for such causes as free transportation on interstate railroads for hoboes who had been promised jobs, minimum wage scales, and shorter work hours.

How also began to publish a newspaper for the hobo community. In May 1913 the IBWA issued *The Hoboes Jungle Scout*, a sheet which later became the *Hobo News*. A potpourri of political essays and stories from the road, the *News* gave many hobo writers their first opportunity to publish.

Although the publication was largely composed of articles on labor problems, testimonies of the exploitation of migrant workers, and political news and theory, it did serve up such tidbits as the following:

HOTEL DE HOBO
HOTEL RULES
No. 1. Board: Fifty cents a square foot.
No. 2. Breakfast at five; Dinner at six; Supper at seven.
No. 3. Guests are requested not to speak to dumb waiter.
No. 4. Guests wishing to rise early in the morning can have yeast for supper.
No. 5. If the room is too warm, open the windows and see the fire escape.
No. 6. If you wish to practice baseball, you will find a pitcher on the stand.
No. 7. If your lamp goes out and you want a light, a feather out of the pillow; that is light enough.

But mostly the newspaper gave How an opportunity to rail against the evils of American capitalism. The articles were anything but panegyrics to the glories of the open road or the edifying commune with nature. Inside those boxcars, How contended, were workers who had been used and swindled, who were up against it and desperate.

Because of his multifarious interests in socialist and radical causes, How received more than a passing interest from federal investigators. At some of the hobo college rallies, military intelligence agents were elbowing FBI men trying to get a look at the infamous "Millionaire Hobo." Numerous reports to the central offices in Washington traced How's movements around the United States and in Europe. Although one agent confused the *Hobo News* with the *Hebrew News*, the investigators did a thorough job of tracing their prey and left a detailed record of How's peregrinations. Typical of their reports are the following comments: "I searched the Howard House used by said How but found only the regular socialist pamphlets. . . . How is shabby and ill-kept, looks like he needs a bath, and probably does, wears side whiskers slightly and gold rim eye-glasses and has an idiotic grin for everybody he meets." The agent's conclusion: "This man I consider dangerous."

In early July 1930, Nicholas Klein, a friend of How and attorney for the IBWA, received a call from the Travelers' Aid Society in Cincinnati that a strange, unkempt man had fainted from hunger and had asked for him. Klein rushed to the train station where the man was waiting. "There, sitting on a bench, stooped, his head bowed, I found my friend. His face was haggard and seamed, his laborer's clothes shabby and torn. I scarcely recognized him." Klein took How home and called a doctor. The diagnosis was exhaustion caused by self-starvation. It was characteristic of How to starve himself during illness, Klein recalled. How gave Klein a will which directed that most of his remaining money be given to the workers of the world, especially for the "education of the disemployed." How died two weeks later of pneumonia in a Staunton, Virginia, hospital at the age of fifty-six. In the weeks following the philanthropist's death, Klein discovered that most of How's fortune had already been spent on the hobo colleges. *The Christian Century* talked of How and his work: "The migratory laborer, he saw, was a detached individual, and many of his troubles, he felt, might be alleviated, if a group-consciousness and some form of organization could be effected. . . . His private benevolences were without number; the sum of them can never be told. It would have been easy for him to have lived comfortably in his north suburban home, and to have established a reputation as a philanthropist by generous gifts to organized charities. But such a course was not for him. He gave himself with his gift." Through the IBWA, his newspaper, his conventions and speaking engagements across the country, How attempted not only to change the image of the American hobo in the public mind but to offer to the workers of the road new outlets for their frustrations and opportunities to gain respect. Happy Dan O'Brien, a swaggering "King of the Hoboes," wrote in the New York *Herald Tribune*, "The world's have-nots have lost a loyal, persistent and selfless friend."

KING JEFF AND THE "HOBOES OF AMERICA, INC."

In 1906, shortly after he had launched his IBWA in Cincinnati, James Eads How was visited by a young, brash road kid who had much the same kind of nose for publicity and organizational drive as the "Millionaire Hobo" and had dreams of his own for a national hobo fraternity. Jeff Davis had run away from his Cincinnati home at age thirteen, ridden the freights to New York where he sold newspapers, and traveled through the jungles and main stems across the country. After making an abortive attempt to form an order of hoboes in San Pedro, California, in 1906, Davis returned to Cincinnati and in 1908, with thirty-two fellow road wanderers, established the Hoboes of America, Inc., a fraternal order which became the most visible hobo organization in the United States. Davis assumed the title "King of the Hoboes," a station he carried for the rest of his life and which he jealously defended against all pretenders.

In the early years of his reign as monarch, King Jeff opened several establishments for his subjects, each euphemistically called "Hotel de Gink." In New York in 1915 he enlisted the cooperation of city officials and rented a decaying five-story building, mobilized troops of ginks to man brooms and shovels, and issued the following edict: "Only real hoboes admitted here; no cranks nor preachers talkin' reform. Any one looking for sympathy will find it in the dictionary under the S's. This is a gent's hotel; don't do nothing you wouldn't do in your own mother's home."

Unlike How's hobo colleges which offered lecture platforms to a broad spectrum of philosophers and political ideologues, Davis's emporiums were designed strictly as havens for the weary travelers, places where a gentleman worker of the road could get a shower, shave, and night's sleep, and could share stories of his pilgrimages with his fellows. "No bugology or socialists, or anarchists" were allowed in these establishments, the King decreed. Davis tried to use his apolitical stance to put him in good stead with local citizenry from whom he wanted to wring contributions—from hand towels to tools, bathtubs to laundry equipment. The New York gink hotel even became proud owner of a piano, and many a night the "loungin' room" swelled with choruses of railroad and hobo ballads.

The gink hotels also acted, if only informally, as employment agencies. Forbidding places, those municipal employment bureaus, Davis noted. "Standin' down there all day waitin' for a guy to sing out your name, maybe 'e does, an' maybe 'e don't, an' no thanks fo' you' pains. Here you can be nice an' comfy, an' then when some nice lady wants the snow shoveled, or a commission merchant's got some stuff he wants moved, we're Johnny on the job." The head of the Seattle organization told of the work among the unemployed: "We took care of the men; the men got two meals a day here; those that worked got three meals—the men that would saw wood or carry wood got three meals a day and the others got two, and then we would place out men as the work came in. We placed a lot of men out among the ranchers here; they got $10 a month, and some $15 a month, from these small ranches and board." When the seasonal jobs were hard to find, Davis and his workers attempted to create jobs—clearing land, wrecking buildings, anything to keep them going.

But most of the Davis agencies, faced with obvious budget problems and often with the antipathy of nearby businesses fearful of their effects on the neighborhoods, were something less than permanent institutions. In New York, his hotel died ignominiously after a single winter.

But if the hotels did not long survive, the Davis organization thrived. Taking a cue from How's IBWA, King Jeff began to hold annual conventions in various cities across the country. He also began to print his own newspaper, *Hobo News Review.* Although Hoboes of America was never a dues-paying organization, it received, thanks to Davis's extraordinary promotional feats, enough contributions to keep it afloat.

From behind his rolltop desk in the small storefront organization headquarters in Cincinnati, Jeff composed a remarkable amount of simple poetry and homespun philosophy proclaiming the dignity of the American hobo and his moral and social superiority over tramps, no-accounts, sots, jungle buzzards, canned heaters, dingbats, geezers, and dopes that some people assumed to be hoboes. Davis once declared, "A hobo is a man who will work when he can get it, at a decent wage, but insists upon the right to beat his way from town to town to better his condition . . . men of good character, not yeggs, crooks or bums." The purpose of his organization, Davis said, was to prevent men who were working on the road from becoming men of this lower sort. A tramp, Davis insisted, believed that the world owed him a living; the bums were either tramps too old to travel or hopeless victims of disease, drug abuse, and "bad pasts." A hobo "keeps to the right of the road and does his best to keep out of trouble. In search of opportunity he travels from place to place hoping to fit in somewhere. He is the greatest optimist in the world and believes the world owes him an opportunity."

The Hoboes of America had an elaborate phalanx of officers including Track Walkers and Jungle Chiefs, Firemen and Engineers, and a Chief Jungle Bull. The publicity-generating Davis enlisted a celebrity membership of nonactive 'boes that included Charlie Chaplin, William O. Douglas, Lowell Thomas, Jack Dempsey, Joe Louis, General Jacob Coxey, Warden Lowes of Sing Sing, Al Jolson, Walter Winchell, Harry Hopkins, and several congressmen, senators, governors, and mayors. If some hoboes were chagrined by the press-agent stunts, other thousands flocked to the banner. They peddled his newspaper, carried his membership cards, rode the rails to the conventions, and took the Hobo Oath:

> I . . . do hereby solemnly swear to do all in my power to aid and assist all those willing to aid and assist themselves. I pledge myself to assist all runaway kids, and to try to induce them to return to their homes and parents. I solemnly swear never to serve as a scab or a strikebreaker against any labor organization, and do all in my power for the betterment of myself, my organization, and organized labor, so help me God.

The Hoboes of America vowed eternal war against the despised vagrancy laws which, Davis insisted, were grossly unconstitutional, imprisoning penniless men in jails, convict farms, peonage camps, and workhouses merely for the crime of being out of work. Men should, if they wish, be free to starve to death, Davis argued, rather than work for cheap scab wages and against the interests of organized labor. Although not as avowedly political in nature as How's IBWA, the work of the Hoboes of America, Inc., nevertheless, was not a frivolous sideshow but a determined effort to combat the plight of migrant laborers. Over the years Davis and his lieutenants lobbied for various programs to benefit the worker, spoke in schools warning children of the curse of the wanderlust, assisted the Red Cross, the YMCA, and the Knights of Columbus in charitable work, and helped army and navy recruiters and sold Liberty Bonds during the First World War. They pushed especially hard for various public works projects which would provide jobs for hoboes.

Jeff Davis, the consummate promoter, kept the whole thing rolling. A reporter in Philadelphia witnessed Jeff's appearance before a labor rally in 1913: "Yesterday, in a witty, snappy speech, switching for moments into pathos and political science, the 'King of the Hoboes' gripped the American Federation of Labor Convention. . . . Gales of laughter greeted his humorous statements, and a sympathetic silence his flights of emotion." Zoe Beckly, a writer for the New York *Evening Mail*, saw Davis as "a born 'Bo Kid.'" Jeff had the quality of "personal magnetism magnified to the enth degree," Beckly declared. "He talks all over. His hands talk, his eyes talk. His gestures are electrical. The magnetic Jeff is full of ideas; a born organizer, manager, leader of men. He could sell an oil painting to a blind man and convince a corporation lawyer that he couldn't 'corp.'"

Although Jeff Davis eventually got married, had children, and bought a car, he continued as supreme monarch of the Hoboes of America, Inc. But the rumblings from other kingly claimants grew more vocal. Happy Dan O'Brien called King Jeff a rank imposter. "Jeff Davis travels by tin lizzie," O'Brien snorted, "No true hobo ever does . . . who ever heard of a hobo with a wife and kids?"

CRUSADERS AND KINGS

As James Eads How and Jeff Davis established national organizations to publicize and ameliorate the lot of the American hobo, others carried on vigorous personal crusades. A man who called himself the "Tramp Evangelist" rode the boxcar-jungle circuit at the turn of the century attempting to persuade wayward boys to return to their homes. Traveling as a typical road wanderer, the Evangelist would take a prushin aside and start talking about the mother and father left behind and the lonely brother and sister. He told a *New York Times* reporter that several hundred had agreed to leave the road.

Rich Eddie Brown, a man wealthy enough to frequent the Waldorf Astoria in New York and the Hotel del Coronado in San Diego, carried on a campaign to establish municipal lodging houses. Rich Eddie would typically drop off his clothes in a hotel and, donning his sidecar Pullman best, head to the main stems to loiter in doorways and beg for handouts. He looked forward to his arrests which gave him a court forum and sometimes an audience with public officials. The plucky Brown hopped freights, worked as a berry picker, and hit the harvests in the Midwest. He permanently damaged his hearing by spending a cold night outside Pueblo, Colorado, on a railroad ash heap, warmed only by the still smoking coals. "Ninety per cent of the men who go on the road are honest men," Eddie claimed. "The itinerant worker is one of this country's great floating assets, and in many cases it is the treatment he receives which changes him from a benefit to society to a menace to society. Arrests for the crime of being broke and charity which rob a man of self-respect both fail utterly to meet the problem he presents." Brown's incognito forays into city skid roads were infectious. After one of his visits to Boston, a former Hub mayor followed the example and slept in that city's municipal lodging facilities. After the experience, he marshaled his political connections and reorganized the institution along lines suggested by Brown. Minneapolis, St. Louis, Denver—all responded to the appeal of Rich Eddie's zealous efforts.

At the same time the Evangelist and Rich Eddie Brown were carrying on their own kinds of campaigns, the hobo kings were after a different kind of notoriety. As the hobo fraternal organizations began to convene annually, some made the election of a hobo king a traditional rite. The circus hoopla and wahoo surrounding the conventions offended some migrant workers and their friends who regarded such festivities as distasteful burlesque on the road workers and a mockery to their dignity. Hood River Blackie, a hobo historian still on the road, considers the conventions and the king coronations offensive and many of those who attend fakes. He refuses to participate. But many hoboes over the years have joined in the annual mayhem. For the hobo showmen the conventions and the elections of kings provided the perfect setting and forum. Here they could spin their stories in the spotlight, with eager reporters and writers taking it all down. Here they could get celebrity attention, however colored.

Although hobo kings were primarily a twentieth-century phenomenon, one individual of earlier years deserves note— General Daniel Pratt, holder of the self-bestowed title "Great American Traveler." Bedecked in a long frock coat and stovepipe hat, the General roamed America for fifty years from the backwoods of Maine to the Indian lands of the West—all the time orating. His topics ranged from "The Vocabulatory of the World's History" to "The Harmonious Vocabulary Laboratory of Government, Considered Physically, Morally, Organically, Oratorically and Sonorously, Especially the Latter." Even before the railroads reached the West, there was Daniel Pratt hitching rides on Conestoga wagons, tramping the freshly marked roads of pioneer families rumbling into Kansas and the Dakotas. The stream of nonsensical non sequiturs became legend as Pratt lectured to farmer and scholar alike. He addressed audiences at Harvard, Yale, and Brown, passing his tattered stovepipe after each florid exposition.

In October 1873, the General perhaps reached his pinnacle. Dartmouth College—whose very halls were permeated with the spirit of America's greatest orator, Webster—welcomed the other Daniel. Preceded by a uniformed marshal and police, with a carpet of flowers strewn at his feet, General Pratt entered the campus in a chariot drawn by two white horses. As he reached the building in which he was to address the students and faculty, the General remarked, "There is my Phantasmagory of the Science of the Universe." The General waxed eloquent that day. One poem was entitled "The Boston Chain Lightning Pandemonium Menagerie of the Plymouth Church." At the end of his address, Pratt was presented with an academic robe and mortarboard with these words: "No Ph.D. will give sufficient tribute to your scholarship, no LL.D. will adequately acknowledge the genius of your requiring cash on the delivery of your lectures. Therefore, in the name of Dartmouth, I hereby grant you the unique and honorary degree of C.O.D."

The most publicity-conscious early hobo celebrity was unquestionably Leon Ray Livingston or "A-No. 1," who once claimed he traveled 526,000 miles on a mere $7.61. After thirty years of roaming the world and chalking his monicker on countless trains, water tanks, and freight sheds,

Leon settled down in Erie, Pennsylvania, in 1914 with a wife, mahogany bed, and silk pajamas. But not before he had spread the word of his road exploits in a series of illustrated booklets carrying such titles as *Life and Adventures of A-No. 1, From Coast to Coast with Jack London, The Snare of the Road,* and *The Ways of the Hobo.* The paperbacks were sold at railroad depots and hawked by news butchers aboard trains. Part fact, greater part fiction, the publications displayed the love-hate, respect-disgust attitudes so familiar in tramp and hobo literature. The road represented challenge, adventure, and manhood; it also represented moral degradation and poverty. Livingston always claimed that his mission was to rescue others from the life that had made him famous. He wrote, "Wandering once it becomes a habit is incurable so NEVER RUN AWAY. STAY AT HOME."

The competition for national hobo sovereignty has raged ever since the birth of the hobo societies. Numerous self-professed hobo monarchs claimed national kingship year after year. The issue was, of course, never settled. No single national convention ever brought together all organizations or all individual claimants to the imperial throne. But one town has tried its best—Britt, Iowa.

The Britt convention was the brainstorm of a few local townspeople who were anxious to promote their community. In 1899, Thomas A. Way and T. A. Potter of Britt had read in a Chicago newspaper that a little hobo club named Tourists' Union No. 63 had elected as officers Onion Cotton of Danville, Illinois, and Grand Head Pipe Charles F. Noe of Sycamore, Illinois. The organization had even published a newspaper called *The Tourists Union Journal* out of the offices of *The Sycamore Democrat* and had held three small previous conventions. The Britt gentlemen invited Grand Head Pipe to come to Iowa for discussions about a 1900 extravaganza, and when the promoters held out the vision of hundreds, thousands of spectators and the national press, Noe was won over.

August 22, 1900: fife-and-drum corps in silly hobo costumes playing ragtime music; banners; reporters from Chicago, Minneapolis, St. Louis, Philadelphia, and Omaha; horse races; barbequed ox; baseball; roulette; many gallons of beer. In the election ceremony at the fairgrounds, Admiral Dewey was elected to the presidency and Philippine Red as veep of Tourists' Union No. 63. Editor W. A. Simkims of the *Britt News* wrote: "It was advertising that Britt was after and she got it."

Some of the 'boes who attended the convention left disillusioned with the blatant exploitation of their brethren. Hundreds of young men in Britt and surrounding areas had come to the festivities with torn clothes, fake whiskers, blackened eyes, dangling tin cans, and some carried pie wrapped up in red-bandana handkerchiefs. Potato Murphy, a legitimate road traveler, was heard grumbling, "Do we ever look like dat? No wonder de dogs chase us." Another stiff walked away from the convention saying that although he was a hobo he had pride.

In 1933, other town leaders of Britt decided to resurrect the hobo convention, and it became an annual affair. Many of the greatest hobo celebrities have made the trek to Britt over the years—Hairbreadth Harry, author of a book entitled *Inner Tubes Come Clean;* Roger Payne, an author with college degrees from both England and the United States; Cannonball Eddie Baker, prune picker and expert slumgullion mixer who in the thirties claimed a national speed train-riding record by covering the Seattle-New York route in seven days; John Prevatil, sign painter and philosopher; Queen Polly Ellen Pep, one of the first hobo queens who was actually a woman and not a man dressed up as one;

Scoopshovel Scotty, who first won the Britt hobo crown at age eighty.

Other hobo celebrities staked their claim from other parts of the country. In the West, Jolly Joe Hamilton enjoyed wide support; in Minneapolis, Joseph Leon Cohen Segal Lazarowitz, D. Mig., D.H.O. (Doctor of Migration and Doctor of Hobo-Ology), long proclaimed himself hobo emperor. Jack Macbeth, dashing, debonair, speaker of three languages, student of ancient Greek, contended for many years that his name alone was sufficient reason to lay claim to royalty— King Macbeth. A dean of the Chicago Hobo College, Jack was an ardent devotee of sun worship. "Out in the Nez Perce reservation," he declared, "I specialized in the influence of sunshine and am now qualified to teach a course of study in the physics and chemistry of light." Jack's claim to kingship was battered in 1932 by rumors of an impending marriage. "Nothing to it," he insisted, "a wife wouldn't be much help out in the jungles and my duties as dean of this institute are too serious to permit me to make love just now."

Happy Dan O'Brien, who had helped Jeff Davis form the Hoboes of America in 1908, argued his own case persuasively. After teaching, boxing, railroading, soldiering, selling, portering, writing, sailing, and preaching, O'Brien had found his true calling in hoboing. The road, with "its scenery, its vast lands, its salmon and trout brooks, babbling by the side of the hill . . . nature and all her charms," was the root of all true philosophy. All editors, he chided the *New York Times,* should have abandoned schooling for vagabondage to give them a broader perspective. The embattled warrior of the road, a veteran of Coxey's Army, had broken nearly every bone in his body in a grueling career. He narrowly escaped death several times and marriage at least six. A small, silver-maned Irishman, O'Brien had organized a bread line in Washington, D.C., in 1929 and for a time was feeding nearly 300 hungry men a day. He attacked another famous Irish hobo, Jim Tully, for misleading the public in the book *Beggars of Life*. The book, O'Brien insisted, described tramps and yeggs and not honest, authentic hoboes who were the most optimistic souls alive. The morose, sullen, vicious brutes so often portrayed in the press and in the writings of Tully and Josiah Flynt were not, O'Brien said, true hoboes.

Jeff Davis, Jack Macbeth, Dan O'Brien—all had their followings. But a ninety-pound hobo from New York spit in all their faces. Ben Benson, the Coast Kid, was perhaps the most colorful propagandist of all. Bennie, who put out his own *Hobo News*, made national headlines in 1937 when he was dragged before a Manhattan court on charges of peddling his paper in Times Square without a license.

Founded in 1936 as a quarterly, the tabloid quickly generated a circulation of 50,000 and was converted to a monthly. A collection of quaint prose, gags, cartoons, line drawings, advertisements for rabbits' feet and novelty items, the journal also featured valuable advice to the road weary: stay out of the South or face the music of jangling balls and chains; hit the Pennsy, Chicago and Alton, Missouri Pacific, Union Pacific, Denver & Rio Grande, and Western Pacific for an easy transcontinental jump; don't mix with tramps, bums, and jungle buzzards or you'll be demoralized. With its racy witticisms and simple philosophical ditties, the *News* had wide appeal on the streets of New York and other cities in the East. Much of the material was solicited from struggling young writers and convicts and the salesmen were mostly 'bo recruits, one of whom was Roger Payne, the hobo philosopher. The office also served as something of a refuge for down-and-out 'boes in the winters.

Ben Benson had been on the road since 1898. On his left arm was a tattooed map of the United States with the words

COAST KID and the initials of his favorite railroad line, the Southern Pacific. In the first part of the century he had traveled the country as a printer, had written poetry for several subterranean newspapers, and had begun to cultivate his particular knack for making himself the subject of newspaper and radio features. Over the years, he roamed the country giving talks on hobo life, proclaiming himself America's most authentic hobo spokesman, and denouncing other fakers and pretenders. He made the Britt convention a number of times and was elected king. But Benson didn't glorify the hobo existence. Although the road was the closest thing to absolute freedom, he said, it was dangerous and debilitating. He had seen men mangled to death, beaten, and made wretched. "I could write for hours about being hounded by the police, about the times I went hungry or about the miserable weather endured. If you knew the discomfort of riding on the top of a fast freight you would agree with me it's no soft life."

In 1917 the superintendent of a public employment office in Minneapolis, an official who dealt with hundreds of men of the road—men who had, like Ben Benson, held down fast freights, dodged police, endured miserable jobs, and watched fellow 'boes fall—told a reporter that the American hobo had been misunderstood. The official said that he often loaned money to hoboes who were temporarily broke or who had been robbed. He never lost a cent. "I am not suggesting that this is good office practice," he said, "but I am saying that there is more manhood in the hobo than many people have believed." With the birth of hobo fraternal organizations and the various activities of hobo reformers, promoters, and writers, the image of the hobo as a worthless, criminal scavenger was under attack. For the hoboes who spoke and listened and argued at James Eads How's colleges, for men who carried the membership cards of Jeff Davis's

Hoboes of America and took part in the hobo conventions, for those who peddled 'bo newspapers and those who read them, there were new outlets for the discontent and boredom and frustration that necessarily shrouded the wanderers of the tracks. Although the road still relentlessly battered those who took it on, the hoboes now had defenders, benefactors, and their own celebrities. Rich Eddie Brown wrote, "I have seen men huddled before offices in the bitterest weather, their pockets and stomachs empty, few of them half-sufficiently clad, but all of them eager to take on any sort of work, no matter how heavy it might be or what the wages. . . . Nine out of every ten of the vast army of wanderers can and will work ably and steadily for their living if they can find and keep the work. It is the tenth man who makes the hardship for the others trebly severe by alienating sympathy from them." Because of Rich Eddie and many others the word was getting out. Ben Benson wrote, "After years of persistent propaganda, through the efforts of myself and others, the word 'Hobo' is becoming to be rather respected throughout the country. Especially is this true in Press reports, in spite of a few Reporters who still regard the Hobo as a tramp, bum, or parasite."

6/ Toward the "One Big Union"

I got a job on an extra gang
Away out on the mountain,
I paid my fee and the shark shipped me
And the ties I soon was counting.

The boss he put me driving spikes
And the sweat was enough to blind me,
He didn't seem to like my pace
So I left the job behind me.

I grabbed a hold of an old freight train
And around the country travelled,
And the mysteries of a hobo's life
To me were soon unravelled.

I travelled east, I travelled west
And the shacks could never find me,
Next morning I was far away
From the job I left behind me.

I ran across a bunch of stiffs
Who were known as Industrial Workers,
They taught me how to be a man
And how to fight the shirkers.

I kicked right in and joined the bunch
And now in the ranks you'll find me,
Hurrah for the cause, to hell with the boss
And the job I left behind me.

—"Mysteries of a Hobo's Life" by T-Bone Slim

NOT WORK BUT PUNISHMENT

THE JOBS—pruning, harvesting, picking, lumbering, plowing, pitching hay, digging trenches, sinking telegraph poles, laying railroad ties, rolling logs, washing windows, shoveling snow—were short-term, hard, low-paying. The stories of the men of the road were usually similar, telling of intermittent periods of work lasting from a few days to a few weeks; brief escapades with booze and women; wandering in search of a new job; hunger; another job; more cycles of work and wandering. They roamed from the mining areas east of the Rockies to the orchards of California to the farm belt of the Dakotas, Wisconsin, Iowa, Illinois, and Missouri to the upper Mississippi lumbering regions. Many days were sagas—waking up hungry, tackling freights in bad weather, grubbing for food, slaving in back-wrenching work. Somehow all the idealistic philosophy about rugged individualism and freedom could seem like so much claptrap when the gut ached and the spirit sank.

One hobo in the twenties told how it was: "Last time I tried a long-stake job, I shipped 'gandy-dancer' with a railroad construction outfit. Shovel stiff, ye know. Guineas! The bunk-car stunk. Oh boy! And shirt-rabbits in the blankets. Say! They made themselves right at home on your hide. . . . Every mornin' I'd turn out and take muh shot of black cawffee, and choke down ye bread greased with sawbelly. Then I'd mosey out and say 'Good mornin' to the pick and 'Howdy' to the shovel, and hop to it." After working on the job a month and suffering various indignities, the stiff pummeled an especially sadistic foreman and beat it on the freights. "When I got back to Los, the bright lights looked so good after that hard life with the gandies, I got drunker than a fiddler's bitch, and blowed all my jack. Two days later I was headed for 'Chi' in a battery-box."

Much hobo labor trekked in a sweep through the Grain Belt. Into the winter wheat harvests of Oklahoma in late May or early June they came, into Kansas and the graingrowing farms of Nebraska, on to the spring-wheat regions of Minnesota and the Dakotas. A harvester might expect a job to last from seven to fourteen days and then he was on to another. After the grain harvest some workers moved into Iowa and Nebraska for corn husking; some hit the sugar-beet factories or the potato fields or headed for the oil fields in Texas and Oklahoma; others freighted to the forests of Montana and Idaho or made it all the way to California and Oregon and Washington. Some hoboes traveled thousands of miles in a year. Many individuals followed consistent migratory patterns year after year; others seemed to move with the shifting winds.

During the prairie wheat harvests, the migration of hobo workers was often so dense that the incoming freights seemed like perches for roosting blackbirds. In the early twenties the Dakota harvest beginning in late July drew upwards of 30,000 workers. Many came from the earlier Kansas and Nebraska harvests, some from industrial towns of the Midwest and lower Mississippi River valley, some from the oil fields, railroad construction sites, and cattle ranches of the Southwest. Many migrants shipped to the Dakotas on their own hook; others were sent by the employment sharks on the main stems of cities such as Minneapolis, Milwaukee, and, of course, Chicago. The hobo poet Bill Quirke wrote an ode to North Dakota:

> *Oft' have I cursed your blizzards, oft' have I damned your heat,*
> *As I hauled your grains to market or threshed it with blistered feet.*
> *Oft' have I vowed to forsake you, never again to come back,*
> *But as spring time is approaching I'm beating down the Track.*
>
> *Why, oh why, do I really sigh for your rolling plains?*
> *And why, oh why, do I long to reap your golden grains?*
> *Though often I have left you, resolved to come no more,*
> *But when summer time approaches, I'm back here as of yore.*

The headline of the Aberdeen, South Dakota, *Daily American* on July 18, 1921, read:

MOVE ON IS ORDER OF POLICE AS TRAINS BRING
HOBO THRONGS TO CITY

Two hundred floating, khaki-clad harvest hands in search of work were intercepted two miles out of Aberdeen by police and forced to march on foot away from town. The town had all the seasonal workers it could handle.

At the same time that law enforcement agents were kicking workers out of Aberdeen, other areas were in desperate need of laborers. Lured by newspaper ads promising high wages, shafted by cunning jobbers and unscrupulous employment agents, sometimes innocently misled by fellow hoboes who had transformed rumors into yellow brick roads, thousands of boomer workers in the harvest seasons rushed around in a helter-skelter frenzy looking for work. It was anarchy, not a system, which matched workers with jobs. It was, most hoboes agreed, senseless. Although state employment agencies aided some employers and migratory workers, most 'boes, in order to land jobs, had to rely largely on their own wits, the hit-or-miss advertising of railroad companies and other employers, and the notorious private employment agencies. Swarms of jobless stiffs passed each other on the freights. While a California fruit crop rotted on the trees for want of pickers, stiffs in Kansas were being herded out of town or vagged. A wheat crop in Nebraska wasted away at the very time itinerant workers in neighboring states went hungry.

When hobo labor was especially scarce during harvest seasons, some local police chiefs, using vagrancy laws as weapons, ordered "roundups" of stiffs from their mission beds and railroad yards. The offer was work in the fields or work on the chain-gang rock piles, a choice between forced labor with bad pay and bad conditions or forced labor with worse conditions and no pay.

Most floating workers had many stories about the sleazy machinations of contractors and their agents. Graft was rife. An agency might get two dollars a head for every stiff delivered to a company. If the agency slipped half a buck to the foreman for every worker landed, it was in the best interest of both to have a rapid turnover of laborers. Wholesale layoffs and hirings meant a constant supply of siphoned funds for the grafters and quick, degrading experiences for the stiffs.

In many cases the workers themselves had to pay fees for the jobs, and the employment sharks often made deals with the employers to divide the money. The employers hired the workers for a short time, laid them off, hired new fee-paying stiffs, and so on ad infinitum.

Once, 4,000 laborers were recruited in Chicago for work in the prairie harvests. The men were charged one dollar each and taken by the company on the trains out of the city to the work site. When they arrived, the head of the crew announced that there were only 350 jobs available at bare subsistence wages, not the higher wages advertised by the employment agency. After 350 men accepted jobs, the other 3,650 were told that they needed the standard railroad fare to return to Chicago. Most didn't have the money and were forced to get back to Chicago the best way they could.

One division superintendent of a western railroad admitted, "It is impossible to get the number and quality of men we need by the offer of a four months' job. So we publish advertisements . . . that read something like this:

Men Wanted! High Wages! Permanent Employment!

We know when we put our money into these advertisements that they are—well, part of a pernicious system of sabotage.

We know that we are not going to give permanent employment. But we lure men with false promises, and they come."
In California railway construction camps in 1914, workers
were on the job an average of only ten days. The old saying
of the agency sharks was thus borne out. It took three crews
to do the work, they said, one coming, one going, one on the
job.

Rexford Tugwell once pictured the migrant lumberman
as a rheumatism-wracked dreg with a dilapidated pack slung
over his diseased frame, haunted by unfulfilled dreams, bitter, resentful. The men who chose to work as timber beasts
in the firs and spruces of the northwestern forests faced iso-
lation, back-splitting work, and harsh conditions. Arriving
in a lumber camp, the worker faced a paradoxical scene, a
cathedral of green lushness formed by mighty 600-year-old
trees and desecrated by the sight and smells of the camp and
its boxcar shacks and foul air.

When a hobo reached a job site, whether in the Northwest
timber regions or in the Kansas prairies, the conditions were
usually unlike anything promised in the company advertisements or the job shark's spiels. One Irish 'bo who had beaten
his way from labor camp to labor camp in the early 1900s,
from the lumber areas to railway construction sites to the ice
fields, called the conditions in most a "hell." "Horses and
cattle are kept more cleaner than human beings in the camps
in the country," he said. Bad food, lousy bunks, outright
fraud in calculating pay, little medical aid for the injured and
sick, lack of water—the camps were grim places. "The
bunks were not fit for a . . . man to live in," another worker
complained. "The vermin nearly ate me up."

The floating workers coined terms for some of the revolt-
ing things they encountered on the road; not surprisingly, a
number were about food. "Canned salmon" they called the
reddish-gray substance that passed for meat; "camp disor-

ders" they called the stomach-wrenching pains and vomiting that often followed a meal of canned salmon. The "belly-robbers" were the commissary men, most of whom, the stiffs suspected, received more money for food from the companies than they invested in the slop that was dished up. Carleton Parker, Secretary of the California Commission of Immigration and Housing, investigated that state's labor camps in 1914. He found deplorable housing and wide-spread, unsanitary, typhoid-inviting conditions—filthy or nonexistent toilet facilities and refuse-strewn grounds.

Although conditions varied somewhat from state to state, industry to industry, company to company, the stories from the road were usually consistent. Fed improperly at company grub tables, fleeced at company stores, housed in miserable company quarters, the road laborers from Wisconsin to California, from the harvest fields to the fruit orchards, echoed similar refrains. "The food was so bad I got sick with it." "The camp was filthy. I couldn't stand the smell." "The meat was rotten. I was afraid to eat it. They told me the company paid for good meat, but the boss was taking his bit out of the contract." One hobo lamented, "Anyone elected or forced to do Hobo work for his daily bread, unless there is something wrong with his 'bean' will admit that the Hobo's labor is not work but punishment, and his life just one darned thing after another." The head of Jeff Davis's Seattle Hoboes' Union charged that the workers on the road were constantly misled, swindled, and cheated. They were placed on jobs through "false representation by the employment office that ships them out to the different work. The men get out there and don't get enough money to get back to where they came from." Some never did get back. In 1911, many 'boes tried to pass the winter in Denver by sleeping in the kilns of a brick-making company. Each evening, with oven fires cooling, the homeless drifters entered the sweltering kilns to take the place of the bricks. Every morning the men were herded out of the kilns to the frigid city streets. A Denver paper noted in January that twenty had died of pneumonia in one week.

PETER SPEEK AND THE FLOATING LABORERS

In 1914, with numerous labor disruptions casting a large shadow over the American economic scene, the federal government, through the Commission on Industrial Relations, began to investigate the cauldron of problems that threatened to boil over into uncontrollable violence and civil disruption. Of the several investigators sent into the field by the Commission, none attempted to come to grips more directly with the plight of the migrant workers than Peter A. Speek. Russian-born, a graduate in sociology from the University of Wisconsin, Speek was conversant in five languages and thus able to mingle as comfortably with many of the immigrant stiffs as with the American-born workers who wandered into the labor camps. A former newspaper editor, Speek had fled Russia after the abortive revolution of 1905 with a life sentence to Siberia hanging over his head. In his work with the Commission he ranged from the camps in Washington and Oregon to the harvest fields of the North and Midwest.

Speek found a large number of skilled workmen among the hoboes—clerks, mechanics, bookkeepers, stenographers, and actors. They had drifted into the hobo battalions for various reasons. Some had wanted to start small businesses and had failed; others had lost money in the stock market, in real estate, or at the gambling tables; some had been wasted by the bottle; others had gotten sick, quit their jobs, and hit the road in despair. Several of the men had been lawyers, physicians, and teachers. In a jungle near Redfield, South

Dakota, in 1914, Speek found, among the 225 men there, twelve who had gone to college, four college students "temporarily on the move," two lawyers, and fifty who had learned a skilled trade.

For over a year Speek traveled among the camps and jungles, noting conditions to which the workers were subjected, gathering detailed personal information about the men themselves, much as the sociological investigator John J. McCook had done in the flophouses and missions of eastern skid-road districts. Many stiffs poured out their frustration and bitterness to Speek and provided a vivid mine of information on their wanderings. One floating laborer had kept a notebook of his summer work in 1913:

1) Farm work	One month	$35 a month	
2) Unloading Oatmeal	One day	$1.50	
3) General Work in Fairgrounds	21 days	7 days; $2 a day	
		11 days; $2.50 a day	
		2 days; $2.25 a day	
		1 day; $1 a day	
4) Cutting wood	5 days	20¢ an hour	
5) Driving team	4 days	$2.00 a day	
6) Laying RR ties	7 days	20¢ an hour	
7) Putting on storm windows	2 days	22½¢ an hour	
8) Varnishing floors	36 hours	22½¢ an hour	
9) Putting on storm windows	4 days	25¢ an hour	
10) Preparing auditorium for charity ball	2 days	14¢ an hour	

In that one year the man had also cut logs, worked in a sand yard, assisted a mason, loaded boxcars, shoveled snow, loaded furniture, washed dishes, plowed, helped build a barn, dug gardens, and beat carpets.

The biographies compiled by Speek are graphic testament to the frantic movement of the road workers from job to job. The two following life histories, of Fred Kiener and Thomas Lee, are typical of the more than 100 he prepared:

FRED KIENER. 29 years. A strong and healthy looking man, decent, orderly, intelligent. Ancestors were Swiss. He was born in America. Single because he never had enough money to support a wife. He had an 8th grade education. His home is in Buffalo. Corresponds with his parents. Does not send money because he never had enough.

He was an apprentice at upholstering for four years then quit on account of the dust; his lungs were weak.

A year ago he was in the Adirondack Mts., N.Y. He found the job himself in building logging cars; 12 hours a day; 13½¢ per hour; slept in Company's shack, board for $4.50 a week. The shack was three stories high; one man in a bunk and 40 men in a small room. The air became so poor over night that the men all felt "doppy," sick and tired. The straw bedding was dusty and lousy; board was provided by the Company, consisted mostly of "canned stuff" and sausage. No privy vaults and surroundings were dirty. Work was hard at times; worked on Sundays. No bathing facilities and nothing provided for recreation. The men were watched and forced to buy from the Commissary Store which had high prices and kept inferior goods. He stayed at this job from September to April; thought this was long enough. He wanted to go and see the world again, he felt "sore all over." When about to leave the clerk of the Commissary Store said he owed $37.00 for a suit of clothes, but he did not own a cent. He was kept two days longer, got his pay and was charged $2.00 for board in these two days; he was glad to get away even with that.

He paid his way to Utica then jumped the freight to Buffalo where he "was all in." Here he joined the Lake Carrier's Association so that he could get work and got a job as a deckhand on a Lake Steamer; work was heavy; slept in the deckhouse which was fair; got $30.00 a month with board—good. Worked 24 days and quit because he never had any proper rest. He was now in Cleveland for a month when he got another job on the deck of "The John W. Keitz" which was nicknamed "The John W. Workhouse" because men were required to work too hard. He was paid $30.00 a month; quit in Duluth because "all in," lost seven pounds. The next two days he "rested" and after two more days he paid $2.00 in advance to a private Employment Office who gave him a job on a Grocery tug, loading the supplies and firing up the boiler. Conditions were the same as on other ships; heavy work; $15.00 a week; prepared meals himself the material of which were furnished by the ship owner. After two weeks quit because he was sick and tired of the work. Next job was on the steamer Norway as deck hand; conditions of labor were fair; pay was the same; quit after 3 months because he wanted a "rest." In South Chicago he began looking for some land job. He applied to a private Employment Office and paid $2.00 and was shipped to Sparta, Wis., where he joined a construction gang replacing steel rails; 10 hours a day; $1.55 a day; board $4.50; slept in a box car on a straw covered floor. The straw was dirty and dusty, but the door was kept open to let the fresh air in. The gang found a man in the same car with sores on his hands which looked like eczema; he was put out and had to sleep in another car. Board was "rotten" and the meat "stunck."

After two weeks he jumped a freight to Minneapolis where he hoped he could be shipped to the west where he might be able to establish himself. After two weeks he paid $4.00 in advance to an Employment Office and was given a slip for his free fare. The conductor refused to let him pass so he returned to the office, but the clerk who had given him the slip was gone until a policeman was called and then the clerk denied that he had made the promise of free shipment. The fees were not returned but another job was promised which he never got.

After several days of waiting and starving he jumped a freight to Grand Forkes, S.D. He looked for work eagerly for two weeks when he boarded another freight on which he met 50 other jumpers going to Poplar, Mont. Here he worked on the Flat Head Indian Reservation, irrigating land for the government; 8 hours a day; $2.85 a day; $4.50 for his board which was very good. After 5 weeks all the white men were discharged because work was almost completed, and only the Indian laborers left.

He jumped a freight to Minneapolis. He was "ditched" a dozen times because the brakemen demanded money from the jumpers when they were returning from the work places, but did not require any when they were going to work; the pay was $1.00 for every division—about 100 miles. If they did not pay they were ditched, beaten or arrested. He was "ditched" only; the brakemen did not dare to beat him, because of his physical strength.

From Minneapolis he jumped a freight to La Crosse, Wis. While sitting in the Railroad station, possibly looking downhearted he was asked by a policeman what he was doing, and in reply he said he was looking for work. The policeman then gave him just five minutes to get out of the city. That night he spent in an old barn. Next morning he found a job at a farmer for a day; pay was 50¢ with his meals.

From here he went to Milwaukee on a freight, and as there was nothing in store for him he jumped again to South Chicago where he got a job laying up a ship for the winter; lasted 5 days; 10 hours a day; $2.16 a day. The next three weeks he slept in ten-cent lodging houses and paid 10¢ per night, during which time he thought he would like some job in a factory during the winter months but all his endeavors to get a job were in vain. His next stop from the freight was at Milwaukee where he has been for two days. Last night he slept in the police station and they told him if he came again they would "club" him or even arrest him.

The laboring people in his opinion ought to get their representatives in Congress. The president cannot do anything without Congress. He thinks laborers are not protected properly by the laws.

He has no future plans. He tried to make good, but all ways have failed. He does not see any way out of the position as a casual laborer.

THOMAS LEE. 58 years; a pretty strong man still; can do hard work preferably outside. Irish. Came to the United States with his parents when he was 5 years old. Single. He could not get the woman he wanted. Homeless, no relatives, no friends. Does not know any trade. When he was 19 years old he started to learn moulding. After a year of learning he discovered that he did not like it. He wanted to drive horses which he liked very much. This is the reason he became a laborer.

He wanted to earn and save money to buy a farm and to start to raise horses, but he always failed. In the periods of unemployment, which often occurs in the position of a laborer, he used up his saved money. After years of struggle, hopes and disappointments, he gave up the idea of becoming a farmer. After that he did not care to save money; when he had it he "blew it in."

A year ago he was in Minneapolis, when he arrived he "rested" a week, drinking mostly beer, going to the shows and to the girls. "A man can't get along without that—it's God's arrangement." When his money was almost gone he got a job through a private employment office; he had to pay his last dollar in advance for fees, and was shipped free to North Dakota into a railway camp replacing ties; 10 hours a day; pay $2 a day; $4 [a week] for sleeping place and board. He slept in a box car, one man in a bunk, bunks two stories high; 10 men in a car, the air was foul; men themselves cleaned the cars, no spittoons; bedding was an old mattress; he cleaned his but others slept dirty. The board was poor—mostly cold storage products; work was pretty heavy; worked Sundays, 15 hours for $3 on a Sunday. After three weeks he quit it; he did not like the heavy dirty work and the poor board. The prices of the goods in the Commissary Store were 30% higher than in the private stores, but the goods were alright as everywhere. Both the store and board were furnished by the Boarding Co.

He went to Mavil, N.D. and hired himself as a helper to a thrasher, who employed 25 men; he worked from sunrise to sun-down—13 hours a day; pay $2.50 a day and board at the farmers', the grubs were good; the men slept in a hay barn, although dusty but clean and without vermin. The work was hard and quite exhausting; the thrasher was a good man. In 16 days the job was finished. He jumped a freight train to Minneapolis. In 2 days he had such a "good time" that from $45 he had only a few dollars left. He then got a job through a private employment office paying $1 in advance. He was shipped free to Duluth to a railroad camp to do surfacing on the Great Northern, 25 miles from Duluth; 10 hours a day, $2 a day, and for camp and board $4. He slept in a box car, one man in a bunk; the bunks were two-story high; 15 men in a car. The air in the cars were foul; every morning the men had headaches and bad tastes in their mouths. There was no man in charge of cleaning the cars; no spittoons; the board was good although cold storage grubs, worked 10 hours a day. He freighted back to Duluth, and "rested" there a week. Every cent was gone. He then got a job through a Boarding Co. who charged him $1 for fees which was afterwards taken off from his wages. The shipment to Hibbing, Minn. was free. The work was in a railway construction camp—surfacing; 10 hours a day; $2 per day; $4 for board; the bedding and board were pretty clean and good. He worked 3 weeks and quit because he earned enough money and wanted to start his journey toward Chicago, where he felt better than anywhere else in the world. He jumped a freight to Duluth; spent one day there—"just having a little time." He then went to Superior and spent another day there. From here he jumped a freight to St. Paul where after he spent a day took a freight to La Crosse, Wis. where he found work in a railway camp, 25 miles from La Crosse; 10 hours a day; $1.75; for board $3.75; slept in an over crowded box car; one man in a bunk; the bunks were two-story high; the bedding was dirty and lousy; he cleaned and cleaned but could not get rid of the vermin. The board was very poor—meats spoiled; he could stand this job only eight days. Went back to La Crosse and spent a day there, then jumped a freight train to Milwaukee—in October. Here he "rested" a week—had just a "little time," did not look for work. The next job he found himself in a railway "extra gang," 14 miles from Milwaukee, raising rails and shoveling earth which was pretty hard work; 10 hours a day; $1.75 a day; $4 for board; the sleeping place, board and foreman were good; he worked one month. The wages were then lowered from $1.75 to $1.65; he and 4 other men: 2 Polish and 2 Irish, quit on account of the reduction. After coming back on a work train to Milwaukee last Dec. 1st, he lived in "Ideal" lodging house, paying 10¢

per night, and 15¢ to 20¢ per meal in restaurants. He will stay here for a few days more, and then jump a freight to Chicago. If he gets hold of anything there he will stay there for the winter and in spring will return to Milwaukee and then to Superior for the purpose of working in the north where the climate is cooler.

He has never asked for public charity. He has done very little begging. In the former times he has stolen money from his friends when they were drunk, but he has left this habit because he was caught and jailed which made more trouble than the money was worth.

He expects a poor winter in getting jobs. He has heard that many factories have reduced their production considerably so that the factory workers are looking for jobs of any kind and pressing upon the common laborer. He has heard that the depression was nothing more than a wall street trick played against the pending currency bill. If this is true he does not know; but he is declined to believe in this explanation of the coming crisis.

He does not know much about labor organizations— thinks they are necessary and good for those only who belong to them. He has never had a chance to join one.

Peter Speek blamed much of the restiveness of the road wanderers on the waning of the American frontier and an increasingly monopolized society that retarded individual initiative. Many of these men on the move looking for work, he concluded, would have staked out a quarter section twenty years earlier. Instead, with the quarter sections rapidly disappearing, with the numbers of drifters swelled by the strains of industrialization and recurrent economic depressions, with no efficient system for matching jobs with workers, the road was not a savior of men but often a destroyer.

It was generally a young man's world that Speek found. Seventy-nine percent of the hoboes he interviewed in 1914 were less than forty years of age; 82 percent had been on the road less than fifteen years. Men did not often become graybeards clinging to brake rods and eating rotten food. As one 'bo remarked ruefully, "We are not interested in old age pensions, because we don't live long enough to get old."

The hoboes were predominately native-born Americans, although some Italians, Poles, Germans, Scandinavians, and Russians were in the ranks. The immigrant classes, Speek concluded, tended to fill the textile mills, stockyards, steel plants, and other industries which offered more or less steady employment and housing areas where their ethnic groups could congregate.

If some stiffs were lured to the road by the siren song of opportunity and promise for a better life, most found it inhospitable. One 'bo told Speek, "We don't bum our way on the railroads, sleep and eat in the jungles and wear poor, dirty clothes because we like to do it. We do it because we can't help ourselves." As the *Hobo News* pointed out, a man could not understand the hobo life and its hardships unless he had been forced to the road by economic pressures, gone hungry, suffered, and, through it all, survived.

The Durst Brothers Ranch, Wheatland, California, August 1913. Twenty-three hundred hop pickers in 105 degree heat were camped in filthy tents, with eight small toilets and no garbage disposal. No water was available in the fields. The lemonade wagon which appeared sporadically among the thirsty pickers was a concession granted to a cousin of the ranch owner. Pay was at the rate of ninety cents per hundred pounds of hops picked. The brothers Durst were particularly careful that all hops be absolutely clean of leaves and stems; only the blooms counted in the payment. The camp grocery store, with its ludicrous prices, paid half of the net profits to the owner. Although many of the pickers were local California casuals and families from the Sierra foothills, a large number were hoboes.

The squalor and fetid conditions of the Dursts' hop fields

were not unique. Similar miserable conditions could be found from the fruit camps of the West to the oyster canneries of the Gulf Coast to the cranberry marshes of New England, wherever unskilled laborers swarmed en masse for short periods of work. To the Dursts and other employers, the conditions seemed adequate for the short periods of time the workers were there. Why provide more expensive facilities for a mass of pickers who would only pass through for a few weeks each year? For the workers, of course, the lice-crawling bunks and rancid food remained a constant; only the places changed. Itinerant workers had been enduring this kind of treatment for many years. Within most of them was a bitterness and anger that festered and cried for an outlet. After investigating the conditions of the migratory laborers in California, Carleton Parker pronounced the sullen and hostile workers "ready to take up political or legal war against the employing class."

ENTER THE WOBBLIES

As a revolutionary organization the Industrial Workers of the World aims to use any and all tactics that will get the results sought with the least expenditure of time and energy. The tactics used are determined solely by the power of the organization to make good in their use. The question of "right" and "wrong" does not concern us.
—from an IWW propaganda sheet

Onward, Christian soldiers, rip, tear and smite!
Let the gentle Jesus, bless your dynamite.
Splinter skulls with shrapnel, fertilize the sod;
Folks who do not speak your tongue, deserve the curse of God.
—from an IWW song

Born in the rough mining camps of the West, the IWW responded to the needs of the frontier working class, a class

powerless, exploited, excluded from craft-union membership. From its first convention in 1905, the theoretical cast of
the Wobblies was toward an industrial unionism which
would bring together all workers regardless of industry and
skills. Big Bill Haywood, at the time an official of the Western Federation of Miners, declared, "We are going down to
the gutter to get at the masses of workers and bring them up
to a decent plane of living."

The preamble to the Wobbly constitution declared a state
of war between workers and capitalists: "Between these two
classes a struggle must go on until the workers of the world
organize as a class, take possession of the earth and the ma-
chinery of production, and abolish the wage system." Wobbly leaders and propaganda literature held out the vision of a
new society in which the "wage slaves" would rise to strike
down their master class oppressors and take over and oper-
ate the great industries of the nation. They would all be
bound together under the banner of the One Big Union—
the "International Industrial Commonwealth."

The call was for sabotage. *Sabotage*—the word itself con-
jured up images of bombs, assassins, of hordes of maniacal
workers dealing death and destruction, of factories and fields
in flames, of a cataclysmic subversion of law and an ordered
society. In the history of the IWW it was usually the Wobs
who suffered vicious acts of suppression and often death at
the hands of their enemies. But it was the Wobbly rhetoric,
perhaps more than anything else, that frightened government leaders, businessmen, any vested interest that saw itself a potential IWW target.

The word *sabotage* derives from the French word *sabot*, a
wooden shoe. Legend says that a workman in France who
became angry at his employer threw one of his wooden
shoes into a loom and knocked it out of commission. The
Wobblies made the wooden shoe a symbol. Some Wobs

called sabotage "deliberate withdrawal of efficiency." Or, as another Wob put it, the workers could "tie up any job tighter'n a cow's ass in fly time."

They also adopted another symbol—the black cat, chilling, mysterious, defiant, the length of claw suggesting terror and power. "No terms with an employer are final," a Wob leaflet proclaimed. "All peace so long as the wage system lasts is but an armed truce. At any favorable opportunity the struggle for more control of industry is renewed." And the organization stood ready to use all force necessary. "The IWW is a fighting organization . . . the progressive program of the IWW by which it will build the framework of a new society within the shell of the old, while at the same time getting ready to take possession of all industries, will be put into effect as fast as possible, whenever and wherever the workers generate the power to do so." The revolutionary industrial union was to be the incipient structure of a new kind of socialist society, free from the pernicious system of wages and the evils of the propertied master class and capitalist government.

The Wobblies made inroads in the early years among the low-paid factory workers of the industrial East. They organized strikes at the Lawrence, Massachusetts, textile factories and in other cities. Fiery agitators Joe Ettor and Elizabeth Gurley Flynn led soapboxing and organizing sorties in the Eastern big cities. But the lasting IWW base would not be in the East but in the camp life of the West.

Some migratory workers such as miners, teamsters, and lumbermen had joined both the Western Federation of Miners, an industrial union formed after the bitter strike in the Coeur D'Alene district in 1893, and the Western Labor Union organized in 1898. When prominent members from these two unions helped form the American Labor Union in 1902, many migratory workers found themselves involved for the first time in radical political causes. Many later joined the infant IWW.

The first Wobbly paper, the *Industrial Worker*, began publishing in Chicago in January 1906. In a series of short articles it contrasted the raw-boned innocence of the hobo with the graft and sniveling pettiness of doctors, lawyers, ministers, law-enforcement officials, and other established citizens. "Red" and "Shorty" were the heroes; American society, represented by the capitalist slavemongers, was the archvillain. As one IWW verse declared:

> The bum on the rods is a social flea
> Who gets an occasional bite,
> The bum on the plush is a social leech,
> Bloodsucking day and night.

But in these early years, most IWW leaders, although aware of and sympathetic toward the exploitation of the army of migratories, were skeptical about the possibility of organizing such a disparate, nomadic mass. Ben Williams, editor of the eastern-based IWW sheet *Solidarity*, talked about the difficulty of organizing the workers of the road in the West: "The people are not there, the industries of the west are yet in the embryonic stage of development only. Furthermore, the workers in the west are constantly on the move. Lumberjacks travel from California to Alaska in a single season; miners, in Montana one month, may be found in Nevada the next." Without legal residence, usually destitute and heterogeneous, the migratories were the kudzu of American labor, tough but uncontrollable.

Some leaders, however, recognized early the IWW potential for mobilizing the migrants. And John H. Walsh, a national organizer for the Wobs and socialist soapboxer who had been actively recruiting on the West Coast, mobilized in grand style. He put together a brass band to attract street-corner crowds, enlisted orators, and began to print and sell cards and leaflets of protest songs, the genesis of the *Little Red Songbook*. Walsh and his wife led a small cadre of calloused harvest workers, lumberjacks, miners, and gandy dancers, dubbed the Overalls Brigade, from Seattle to the fourth annual IWW convention in Chicago. As the Brigade set out from the Portland railroad yards on September 1, 1908, each man, Walsh recalled, was "dressed in black overalls and jumpers, black shirts and red ties, with an IWW book in his pocket and an IWW button on his coat." With the men beating their way on freights from town to town, the Brigade held open-air jungle meetings and sold literature along the route. Along highways and railroad sidings, in fields crowded with men out of work, they sang.

> *Oh, I like my boss,*
> *He's a good friend of mine;*
> *That's why I am starving*
> *Out in the bread line.*
>
> *Hallelujah, I'm a bum,*
> *Hallelujah, bum again;*
> *Hallelujah, give us a handout*
> *To revive us again.*

The Wobblies survived an agonizing period of internal division and bickering, much of it over the issue of the role of politics and the Socialist Party in the union. After a bitter 1908 convention in which the proponents of "direct action" assumed control from those favoring a more cautious, political approach, many men walked away from the union never to return. In the ensuing period of readjustment, with its numbers depleted, the IWW increasingly turned to the itinerant timber beasts, harvesters, and miners, those workers that many Wobbly leaders now felt constituted a natural constituency. The *Industrial Worker* ran the following editorial on December 22, 1910:

WHAT IS A HOBO

The capitalist press says it is a fellow who is out of work, and that he is harmless except that he burns up ties along the railroad to keep warm. So he is a man OUT OF WORK, caused by the industries being shut down. Glorious! We thought he was some fellow who would not work, but was a kind of PROFESSIONAL BUM and petty thief that preyed on others. A HOBO and a TRAMP are nice names to have the boss calling you after he has worked hell out of you and taken the greater share of the production of your toil. . . . It's up to you. One union for all is the only cure. COME IN.

But Wobbly success among the migratories was frustratingly slow. Many hoboes were undoubtedly intimidated by the unwarranted reputation of the IWW as a crazed, bomb-throwing gang of thugs; other stiffs were leery of labor organizers generally who, they thought, were shyster con men out for the fleece; other 'boes merely wanted to be left alone. Three months after the appeal for hobo laborers appeared, the frustration over the slow response of the road workers to the IWW message spilled onto the front page of the *Industrial Worker*. A half-page cartoon under the masthead pictured a bindle stiff, pipe in hand, marching along a track. The caption read, "HE SAYS THE IWW IS TOO D———D RADICAL."

But the Wob effort among the migratories intensified. IWW newspapers began to carry an increasing number of articles on lumberjacks, harvesters, pickers, smeltermen, and gandy dancers. The IWW halls became social centers where, as Carleton Parker noted, the stiffs could "find light, a stove, and companionship." At some of the union halls the 'boes could even see motion pictures for a five-cent admission charge. Wob "camp delegates" roamed through job sites and, armed with red cards, pamphlets, and songbooks, they recruited and mobilized strike actions.

Big Bill Haywood explained that the Wobblies were going

to help establish "community life in the jungles." Wob camp delegates were to organize committees to keep the camps clean and sanitary, help rustle the towns for work, and clean out the jungle buzzards and scissorbills. The Wobs were to make the hobo jungles their own and weld a loose fraternity with a solder of union spirit. From street-corner and grain-field pulpits came the vision—the great dream of the new society, the revolution, Valhalla, when the lordly parasites were overthrown by the united working force, when the tools of production were finally controlled, not by the capitalist devils, but by the people. One stiff who joined the Wobs recalled a winter night in Seattle in 1912 hearing a soapboxer on skid road: "It wasn't long before I was drinking in the message of a great hope, a plan of freeing the world from economic slavery, so amazing in its simplicity that it dazzled me." Infused with the call, the drifter signed up, freighted to North Dakota for a free-speech fight, joined in a hunger strike, and marched off to jail for spreading malicious propaganda.

As the Wobbly campaign gained momentum, IWW leaders began to attack and ridicule other organizations which they feared were siphoning off support for the union from the hobo community. Although James Eads How's organization of hoboes, the International Brotherhood Welfare Association, was not essentially a labor union but a fraternal society, and although How had encouraged hoboes to support the labor movement, IWW leaders saw fit to attack him as a "faddist" with half-baked schemes likely to injure the hobo cause rather than help it. That IWW leaders felt obliged to attack How was a measure of his influence among the hobo community, an influence which Wob leaders saw damaging their own recruiting efforts. How's publicity campaign and his wistful political entreaties for the eight-hour day, free transportation to work sites, and a national

employment bureau were nothing more than flights of
fancy, the *Industrial Worker* charged in 1911. Only
through agitation and strikes, only through seizing and
wielding power, the Wobs insisted, would the capitalist
vipers be humbled. "WE WANT NO CHARITY," the *Worker*
declared. "WE ONLY WANT WHAT WE CAN TAKE BY OUR
MIGHT."

Much of this Wobbly might was to be marshaled, not
with physical violence as IWW rhetoric implied, but
through song. An *Industrial Union Bulletin* editorial in
1908 had emphasized the significance that music would play
in the labor crusade. "What more powerful to excite ridicule
than a comic song?" The charity house ministers, the sky
pilots, the *Bulletin* charged, had been peddling their tripe
for too long, promising a better next world while picking the
pockets of the poor in this one. "Oh, that some new Rouget
de Lisle would write us a fitting song to express our hopes
and rouse our often flagging energies," a Wobbly editorial
declared. Joe Hill was no Rouget de Lisle but he more than
answered the call.

A Swedish immigrant who arrived in America in 1901,
Joe Hill joined the IWW about 1910 and in the five years
that followed became the musical inspiration for the Wobbly crusade. Along with Ralph Chaplin and Matt Valentine
Huhta (T-Bone Slim), Hill stands as one of the most in-
fluential composers of labor songs in the twentieth century.

Hill's genius was in setting the tunes and hymns of the
day to lyrics of radical Wobbly protest and to the discontent
of the common working stiff.

> Now the boss the law is stretching, and bulls and pimps he's
> fetching,
> They are a fine collection, as Jesus only knows.
> But why their mothers reared them, and why the Devil
> spared them

Are questions we can't answer where the Fraser River flows.
Where the Fraser River flows, each fellow worker knows,
They have bullied and oppressed us, but still our union grows.
But we're going to find a way, boys, shorter hours and better pay, boys,
And we're going to win the day, boys, where the Fraser River flows.

As the IWW pressed for converts on the streets, their proselytizers took on the tactics of the Salvation Army (the Starvation Army, the Wobblies called it) and other religious charitable organizations. When the Salvation Army launched its anti-booze drive in the slums of nineteenth-century England, its songwriters put religious words to popular songs of the day and drew crowds to open-air meetings with street-corner bands. The Wobs began to do the same thing and many main-stem locations became battlegrounds with the Wobbly Industrial Band taking on the Sally bands. Often the Wobblies would counter Sally religious tunes with union parodies of the same music. To the strains of "In the Sweet Bye and Bye," for example, came the IWW song "The Preacher and the Slave."

Utah Phillips, IWW organizer, songwriter, and singer, recalled one of the ploys used by Hill and T-Bone Slim to attract audiences. They would hide in an alley while a Wob shil, sportingly dressed in businessmen's clothes, walked toward them. As he reached the alley, he would suddenly start yelling that he had been robbed. As the inevitable crowd gathered around, someone would ask who robbed him. The shil would respond with something like the following: "I've been robbed by the capitalist bloodsuckers." This was, of course, the cue for the band to emerge from the alley and break into a song. One favorite was "The Tramp," a lament that tells of a stiff looking for work in the dreary city and the response he gets from housewives, preachers, cops, judges, and, finally, even Saint Peter himself:

> *Tramp, tramp, tramp, keep on a-tramping;*
> *Nothing doing here for you.*
> *If I catch you 'round again*
> *You will wear the ball and chain—*
> *Keep on tramping, that's the best thing you can do.*

Joe Hill wrote songs at strike sites and wrote others on request from picketers thousands of miles away. Many of the ditties were slightly modified to fit the particular occasion and thus became known as "zipper songs"—old words could be zipped out and new ones zipped in.

Hill even turned the American hero Casey Jones into a union scab. Apparently written during a 1911 strike of shopworkers on the Southern Pacific in San Pedro, California, the song was an attack on engineers who kept the trains rolling while others manned the picket lines:

> *Casey Jones kept his junk pile running;*
> *Casey Jones was working double time;*
> *Casey Jones got a wooden medal,*
> *For being good and faithful on the SP line.*

Joe Hill became a Wobbly martyr. Jailed on trumped-up charges of murder, he was executed by a Utah State firing squad on November 19, 1915. His songs have been kept alive in more than thirty editions of the *Little Red Songbook* published by the IWW, revived again and again by picketers and protesters, and recorded in albums by numerous folksingers. Pete Seeger wrote recently, "From time to time in recent years, the November 19 anniversary of Joe's execution has been memorialized with a program of his songs. They bring his presence close. To the singers it must seem as though he peered over their shoulders occasionally, with a grin creasing his features as though to say, ' 'Pears to me you're making a lot too much fuss over me, personally. But if it helps organize the OBU [One Big Union], go to it, Brother!' "

By 1912 the songs and agitating had spread the message of industrial unionism to migratory workers across the country. Although the IWW could not claim large numbers of fees-paying recruits, the Wobs had nevertheless made many hoboes aware that an organization now stood ready to fight the bums on the plush.

In August 1913, the hundreds of migrants mired in the wretched living and working conditions of the Durst Ranch in Wheatland, California, rebelled and undertook direct action. Led by Wobbly agitator Richard "Blackie" Ford and others, the migrants held meetings, sang Joe Hill songs, and asked for more toilets, free water in the fields, lemons instead of acetic acid in the lemonade sold by the field concession, and other demands. Instead, they got a sheriff, deputies, and a posse.

A few minutes after the sheriff and his band rode into the hop yards, four were dead: two law-enforcement officials and two in the crowd including a young boy. Many lay injured. The next day, deputies began arresting several workers on charges of inciting a riot. One of the first arrested was one Harry Bagan, suspected of being the secretary of the strikers' meetings. Bagan, it turned out, couldn't read or write. Another, Otto Enderwitz, was identified as the man who was translating speeches into Spanish. Enderwitz couldn't speak Spanish.

All over the state of California deputies and detectives roamed in the following days, slapping John Doe warrants on migrants and IWW organizers and throwing them into jail. In subsequent trials two Wobs were convicted of murder and sentenced to life imprisonment although evidence at the trials indicated that all the Wobblies at the ranch had consistently counseled nonviolence. Predictably, the state newspapers featured stories on Wob terror and sabotage.

In this case, as in the entire history of the IWW, Wobbly rhetoric on class war and direct action fueled the image. Although public attitudes toward the Wobs may have been damaged by the riot, among the western migrants there was new respect and enthusiasm. Paul Brissenden, who investigated the California labor system for the Commission on Industrial Relations in 1914, claimed that several thousand had flocked to the Wob banner in California. One organizer told Brissenden, "Three or four years ago I had a hard time to get those scissorbills working stiffs to even listen to the IWW dope. Now it's easy. They come around and ask for it." In the following years, IWW-led strikes and agitation resulted in some solid gains for the migrants in much of the West and, as it had done after Wheatland, solidified support for the union among the workers.

In April 1915, Big Bill Haywood convened a conference in Kansas City to work out an IWW harvest field program. At that meeting the delegates formed the Agricultural Workers' Organization and opened an intensive drive for members in the Kansas and Oklahoma harvest belt. Pushing for a minimum wage of three dollars an hour, a ten-hour day, and other traditional porkchop demands, Wobbly organizers trudged tirelessly through the jungles and labor-distribution centers trying to reach workers who had rarely, if ever, been approached by a union representative. They attacked the labor bureaus and employment sharks. They urged the men to hold out for higher wages and implored the working stiffs to fight the system. One IWW leader declared, "If a man is treated like a dog he's a fool if he don't bark, ain't he?"

Wobbly tactics in signing up members were hardly subtle. Armed with pick handles, recruiters took over trains entering harvest regions, and some 'boes complained of intimidation. A red card ensured safe passage; lack of a red card might brand the hobo a scissorbill and get him thrown off or worse. One hobo remembered a buddy flashing an American Legion card instead of the red card. He was told to use it for toilet paper and wise up or find himself on the cinders. Although some old-time Wobbly leaders complained of the increasing use of strong-arm tactics to force 'boes to sign up, the campaign rolled on with full force and effectiveness. In Oklahoma, Kansas, and the Dakotas, organizing committees swept into the camps and the jungles. Some freight riders were merely buying protection when they handed over money for the cards, but the membership swelled as did the union treasury. Wobbly leader Ben Williams said that 1915 was the first year the IWW had ample funds, enough to open a large office as general headquarters on West Madison Street in Chicago. Besides the Grain Belt, the IWW began to claim new success in organizing lumber workers in Washington, Idaho, Montana, and in the Midwest and among the metalliferous mining camps of the North and Southwest.

In 1916, with the First World War creating great demands on the American farmer and on other industries serviced by hobo labor, the IWW continued to make substantial progress as numerous Wobbly-led job actions achieved higher wages and better working conditions. But many communities, recognizing the success of the IWW, began to make concerted efforts to wipe out its influence. The war made it easy.

IWW leaders were openly hostile toward American participation in the war. They opposed the draft, calling it a capitalist effort to fill the pockets of "the blood-puddlers of the Oligarchy" at the expense of the cannon-fodder workers—"to drag workers against their will into a war in which they have nothing to gain and to force them to fight with other workers with whom they have no quarrel . . . to compel them to suffer privation and encounter death, diseases, and mutilation on the blood-soaked fields of France, or to starve themselves at home in order that the capitalists in this country may amass fortunes by feeding Europe." This was a war, Wobblies claimed, to crush Prussianism abroad while Prussianism ran amuck at home. *Solidarity* ran an article in April 1917 denouncing the "river dog" Samuel Gompers and his American Federation of Labor for their support of the war. "Gompers can no more speak for American labor," the paper declared, "than a jackass could speak for a nightingale."

The Wobbly position, of course, played into the hands of local organizations variously known as "State Councils of Defense," "Security Leagues," and "Committees of Public Safety," formed for the more effectual prosecution of the war. These organizations and other commercial clubs and town trade organizations, usually made up of bankers, real-estate agents, and other businessmen, were determined to sniff out traitors and disloyal citizens in their midst. The Wobblies were not hard to find. In several cases, groups of Wobs in the Plains states were taken to the fields, stripped, and beaten. But vigilante violence was only a supplement to official suppression. Under state criminal syndicalist laws, many Wob leaders were jailed and run out of towns. And in June 1917, the federal government indicted the top leadership of the IWW. In the months that followed, their replacements were continually harassed and arrested. Wobbly newspapers were suppressed and union halls closed down. The climate was definitely not favorable for exponents of left-wing philosophy or anything that smacked of it. In 1919, for example, an FBI agent arrested a forty-two-year-old Ital-

ian-American named Angelo Macetta in Boston for selling a
hobo newspaper on the streets. After a long interrogation in
which Macetta tried to demonstrate that he had no bombs
and was not a lunatic subversive, the nervous agent remained unconvinced and reported to the Washington home
office that he was "impressed with the cleverness and
shrewdness of subject which is way beyond the innocent ig-
norance that he was trying to show before us." This incident, not unlike numerous others in this period, occurred in
the same year that a man was arrested in Detroit for reading
George Bernard Shaw's *An Unsocial Socialist* on a street-
car.

The IWW General Defense Committee estimated that at
the beginning of 1920 more than 2,000 Wobs were in jail for
sedition, disloyalty, criminal syndicalism, and vagrancy.
The IWW survived the suppression. But the loss of leadership and the enervating succession of trials and costly defense efforts robbed the union of its prewar organizing zeal,
and the Wobblies never regained their strength.

Many hoboes had certainly not shared the ideological positions of the IWW. Thorstein Veblen, investigating the
farm-labor situation for the Food Administration in 1918,
found, for example, that the average working stiff in the harvest fields of Missouri, Iowa, Minnesota, and the Dakotas
did not share the antipathy of the Wobbly leadership toward
American involvement in the war. Many 'boes thought little
about the IWW vision of revolution and a postcapitalist
America. And some hoboes had been driven into union
membership by force and intimidation and had bought red
cards more out of fear than conviction. But for large numbers of American hoboes the IWW had a lasting impact.

Unstable, rebellious, aggressive, freewheeling—the IWW
seemed to be always on the move, dynamic, like the hoboes

themselves. Its crusade fervor incited festering class hatreds among the road workers. If much of its spittoon philosophy seemed like sophistry to some, it at least sounded good to weary stiffs who had taken years of battering on the road. In numbers of cases, workers had seen IWW porkchop agitation produce higher wages and better working conditions. The Wobs had taken on the damnable system and, in many cases, left it upturned. Bill Haywood's promise to go "down to the gutter to get at the masses of workers" had not been mere hyperbole.

At the same time Wobbly influence was waning because of wartime purges, the face of American labor on the road was also changing. As industries in the West, especially lumbering and grain production, adopted more sophisticated equipment, as the population in the West increased and employers tapped more and more home-guard labor, as many workers took to the highways in flivvers and left the life of the jungles and the freights behind, the influence of the American hobo was also waning. But the years of the red card and the strikes and the songs and the marches had been stirring ones. And even in the twenties, even with the glory days of the movement behind, much of the spirit was still there. Len De Caux, a British-born, Oxford-educated, long-time figure in the American labor movement, spent his early years in the twenties beating his way as a hobo harvester to taste some of the life of the working class. He recalled the spiel of a Wob camp delegate on a freight near the North Dakota border. "Take this harvest," the Wob said, "If we're organized, we don't have to work for no lousy three or four bucks a day . . . if we don't like the grub, we don't get sick on it. We ask Farmer John real polite to do better. If he says to go suck ourselves, we just say: 'Okay, we won't work . . . and you won't get a man from the jungles or the freights.

They're all carrying Red Cards like us.' " Ralph Chaplin's "Solidarity Forever" had said it best:

> It is we who plowed the prairies; built the cities where they trade.
> Dug the mines and built the workshops; endless miles of railroad laid.
> Now we stand, outcast and starving, 'mid the wonders we have made;
>> But the Union makes us strong.

7/ Big Chi

Bᴵɢ Cʜɪ—the hub of the nation's rails, the migrant mecca, Hobohemia. For the 'boes all roads, it seemed, led to Chicago. No American city was so accessible by freight; hundreds thundered in and out every day in the early part of the century. Chicago—the center of a giant steel web that spread its latticework to every corner of the nation, an industrial titan, shuttling cattle and homeless men.

London had its Commercial Road; Paris, its Haute Montmartre. In Chi it was West Madison Street, the nation's consummate main stem. The West Madison area had once been a haven for the upper crust, with marble-fronted residences, spacious boulevards, and manicured lawns. In the wake of the Great Fire, which drove the wealthy to greener meadows, came West Madison's new look—dilapidated tenement houses, shabby hotels, sleazy bars, and an army of hoboes, tramps, and bums.

Walk along West Madison today and only the skeleton remains. Most of the missions are boarded up and only broken signs dangle as reminders. Many of the buildings have vanished, victims of urban renewal. A few down-and-outs still shuffle along, but only the very few remember the teeming days of West Madison's glory and infamy. The old jungles around Grant Park have long since disappeared, just memories to surviving 'boes, such as Hobo Bill, who once flopped on the lake front minutes from the Loop. The State Street office of Ben Reitman, Chicago's hobo celebrity, is now occupied by an accountant.

Just across the bridge from Chicago's business district, the Daily News Building once stood as a dubious beacon, the gateway to a netherworld. Up Madison from Canal to well beyond Racine was a concoction of missions and other establishments for transients where a homeless man could get a cheap night's rest. Here were the private employment agencies, the so-called slave markets, where the workers scanned the signs and chalk-scribbled windows for word of jobs hundreds, thousands of miles away. Here the men could mingle with comrades and swap information from the road. Here were the greasy spoons, the Salvation Army recruiters, the shysters, crooks, petty thieves, whores, jackrollers, soapboxers, fortune tellers, pickpockets, hopheads and their pushers, sexual perverts, and tomato-can vags.

In no other city did the hobo find more complete winter accommodations. The eateries, lodging houses, secondhand clothes stores were all congregated in a few square miles, all catering to his special needs. But along with essential services that brought food, shelter, and clothing were other establishments and other hustlers and other cons vying for his winter stake—the prostitutes, thieves, dope dealers, and bars. It was all there. And from 300,000 to 500,000 migrants and other homeless men passed through the hobo capital each year in the twenties and thirties.

The 'boes knew the layout well. To the west along West Madison were the haunts of the employment bureau "man-catchers." Ralph Chaplin remembered "the streets swarming with migratory workers resting up between jobs or ready to ship out—loggers, gandy dancers, lake seamen, harvest hands ... every freight train that reached Chicago dumped jobless odd-job workers on the already crowded 'skid row.' " Jobs for muckers and skinners, steam shovel operators, cooks, timber beasts, rock miners, teamsters. Ship out to Grand Rapids or Butte or the West Coast, transportation provided "on the cushions," small fee required. The veterans knew and despised the petty graft of the sharks; knew that some of the jobs they might accept could be non-existent or scab or of planned short-duration to guarantee a steady stream of fee-paying workers; knew of the secret deals between contractors and foremen and employment agencies to split the take, all of it at the expense of the poor stiffs who wandered the West Madison corridor.

South of Madison was the neon of State Street, "Bum's Broadway," the playground with its tawdry burlesque houses, penny arcades, bookies, and beer joints—numberless beer joints. Here were the ragged prostitutes whose own status was reflected in their clientele.

North along Clark Street were rows of pawnshops and secondhand stores where the wanderers could pick up such necessities as worn-out suits and pieces of battered leather that passed for shoes. Also to the north was the intellectual center, Washington Square, or "Bughouse Square," the Latin Quarter of Hobohemia, with its agitators and thinkers, dreamers and philosophers, vagabond poets and revolution-ists—all filling the "village" with soapbox messages. On summer Sundays Bughouse stirred with life. Hoboes talked with Russian tearoom philosophers; free-love proselytizers argued with religious proselytizers; soapboxes became stages for Marxists and Calvinists; Wobblies and anarchists ha-rangued passers-by on street corners. Denizens of the Blue Fish and the Dill Pickle, bohemian intellectual emporiums, talked of politics, economics, and art. To the hobo this was a welcome antidote to the mundane. If some couldn't match intellectual wits with one of their loquacious brethren, they could at least listen. One 'bo said he loved the writings of Kipling, Bret Harte, the poems of Swinburne, the Social Darwinist philosophy of Herbert Spencer. "I don't savvy all that those old coots write," he admitted, "but I like to wras-tle with 'em just the same."

To the east was the Grant Park idling resort, the loafing center where the homeless could loll in the grass reading, talking, killing time. Along the shore from the Field Museum northward were the jungles where in good weather the men could sleep in improvised shacks and fish at no expense.

The quality of food on the stem deteriorated from poor to worse with the price. If a 'bo could cough up twenty-five cents for a meal, he could eat relatively well at the two Meyer Jacobson taverns, the Tile Grill, and the Wheel Cafe. Down the stem, the Penny system, which operated hobo restaurants in many large cities, had "specials" for three cents and up.

A 'bo with money could sleep in the luxury accommodations, usually hotels with private beds in small cages. Price: thirty-five to fifty cents a night. One such establishment at 623 W. Madison was called Workingman's Palace, an apt if not accurate title. One hobo remembered a night in Chicago with no cash in his pocket but a jug of wine for consolation. Lying in a vacant lot next to the Palace, he hears a great thud next to him but thinks nothing of it. Weird noises are commonplace on the stem. Later in the night he wakes up and discovers a man lying next to him and offers the guy a swig of what's left in the jug. The guy doesn't answer. In the morning, as he wakes up with a half-cleared head, the 'bo discovers that his neighbor is dead. Two cops investigate and find that the man had been drinking wine with other guys on the fourth floor of the Palace and suddenly announced that he was going to jump—which he did. He missed our friend on the ground by inches. "Boy, he was all fucked up," the survivor concluded. "That happens down there every day on that skid row."

Further on down the stem were such hotels as the Fremont with its scruffy sleeping lofts for twenty-five cents a night. For less money, ten to fifteen cents, the flophouses of-

fered common sleeping areas. Hogan's Flop was perhaps the
best known. The original Hogan, a Spanish-American War
veteran and boomer railroad worker, was long dead when
the sociologist Nels Anderson walked incognito into
Hogan's in the early twenties to see the conditions for himself. One man who patronized Hogan's told Anderson that
although old man Hogan had died, the bugs that had been in
business with him lived on. "You have to know where
Hogan's is to find it," Anderson recalled. "A narrow, shaky
stairs, a squeaky door, a feebly lighted entrance, a night clerk
who demands a dime and you are within ... the air was
stuffy, the light dim. I walked around the room looking for a
place to lie down. Dozens of men were sleeping on the floor
with their heads to the wall. Some were lying on paper,
others on the bare floor. Some were partly covered by their
overcoats; some had no overcoats. It is an art to curl up
under an overcoat. One man of fifty years or more had re-
moved his shirt and trousers and was using the latter for a
pillow. He had tied his shoes to his trousers which is evidence that he knew 'flop' house ethics." Anderson, who tried
to sleep on the floor, left the flop at two-thirty in the morning marveling at the endurance of the men of the road. The
snores, spitting, coughing, hard floors, and bugs had been
too much for the sociologist, who had himself been a man of
the road in earlier years.

The penniless man, alone in Chicago with no place to stay
or nothing to eat, often turned to the rescue missions, especially in very cold weather. From the Holy Cross Mission
(Catholic) to the Cathedral Shelter (Episcopal) to the
Christian Industrial Mission (Presbyterian), the men could
get coffee, a little food, and a flop. The Good Will Industry
offered, as some of the missions did, delousing facilities with
their desinifying sermons.

The public facility, until it closed in 1917 because of political bickering, lack of funds, and inefficient management, was the Municipal Lodging House, or, as one man referred to it, "Chicago's gift to its penniless toilers." Just off the arcade of cheap saloons, cafes, and murky playhouses, the Union Street establishment was shrouded in an almost black street. "With fear and difficulty," one lodger recalled, "I found an old shell of a building. Arriving too late for a bed, I was allowed to lie down with sixty others, from boys of fifteen to old men of seventy, on the floor. In the foul air, unwashed, unfed, with my shoes for a pillow, with aching limbs, I endured, until day break." One somber bit of irony struck the 'bo. Nearby was the magnificent railway station, an edifice which, in its grandeur, represented to him the power and might of the American railroads. On the steps of the station, destitute men begged for pennies, men whose lives had been twisted and tormented by the railroad, the haunting steel carpet.

Many men perished on the curbs and in the alleys and gutters of West Madison. In a 1930 blizzard they found minstrel blues singer Blind Lemon Jefferson frozen to death. His "Tin Cup Blues" had said it all:

> *I stood on the corner and almost bust my head*
> *I couldn't earn enough to buy me a loaf of bread ...*
> *The tough luck has struck me and the rats is sleepin' in my*
> *hat.*

For many like Blind Lemon the main stem brought an inglorious, undignified, unmourned end. But thousands kept coming. They ambled along, gazing vacantly in store windows, wandering into used bookstores to check out back issues of *Esquire*, *Adventure Stories*, and *Wild West*, swapped tales with pushcart hawkers, heard pitchmen peddling their messages and their patent medicines, elixirs, tonics, and soaps. Many scanned copies of *Billboard*, the sheet that covered the legitimate stage, nightclubs, radio, burlesque, circuses, and carnivals. Some of the men on the stem had worked the carnies and fairs and knew circus performers personally.

The men might drop in at the Proletariat at 1237 West Madison, Daniel Horsley's glorified bookstore. A former miner who retired after too many doses of foul air or the "black damps," a student of Marxism and a soapboxer, Horsley offered many free services to the homeless community at the little shop—mail collection, safe deposit for personal possessions, and occasional free books.

The 'boes might stop to see Charley Langsman, the best-known mission director on the stem. A former tramp, Langsman ran the Bible Rescue Mission, notable because it fed men the year around. Charley's free picnics in the country were memorable galas, with the men of West Madison riding out of the city en masse in trucks furnished by various merchants in the area.

The wanderers could stop and chat with former wanderer Gabby, an old-time hobo who had traded in life on the road for street peddling. Gabby sold can openers, unbreakable combs, and a mysterious mixture to remove stain from clothing. A poet for the *Hobo News*, Gabby carried wrinkled clippings of his verse in his pockets. He had spent time in the slammer for selling without a license and, while there, wrote the song "The Cook County Jail," something of an ode to bedbugs. An excerpt:

> *They were crawling on the ceiling, on the sidewalks and the floor,*
> *They were falling in the toilet singing "Pull, boys, for the shore."*

The men could visit the local headquarters of the IWW where Wob recruiters labored to sift the worker from the streams of derelicts, gamblers, and grafters milling up and down Madison.

The men could walk to 7th and State to the welcome sign, "Mother's Restaurant. Don't Go Hungry, See Mother." This was Lena "Mother" Greenstein's refuge for the homeless. In the hard days, they would line up by the hundreds for a cheap or free meal. And the old-timers heaped praise on the cooking. Better, they insisted, than the dishes at the Blackstone or Drake hotels. Not once, the 'boes would say, had Mother turned anyone away empty-handed. Something of a Chicago legend, Mother Greenstein ran a kind of hot line for homeless in trouble, referring the jobless to the employment offices, the sick to the Health Department clinics, the dirty to the Municipal Lodging House, and the hungry to the various charities. One of her circulars read, "Cheer up. Everyday there are a thousand new jobs looking for men, and there are hundreds of men and women who want to serve God and Humanity by helping needy folks. Don't despair, don't hate, don't try and forget your misery in booze, vice or crime. Be a man. Try harder. You can succeed. You can help build a world without unemployment, misery, hate and wrongdoing, and avoid the human scrapheap."

Each Thanksgiving, Mother Greenstein threw a free dinner she called The Feast of the Outcasts and invited not only the migratory workers but "reformed hi-jackers and jackrollers, unsuccessful rumrunners and bootleggers, former black-handers and white slavers, habitual booze-fighters and dopes, unlucky ex-cons and ex-gunmen, the handicapped, the mistreated, the wornouts, disappointed agitators, soapboxers and spittoon philosophers, and all the down-and-outers whom the government, society and the church have forgotten this day." That guest list just about covered the wanderers of West Madison Street and, at one time or another, Mother hosted them all.

CHICAGO'S HOBO CELEBRITY

One of Mother Greenstein's closest friends and mutual benefactors of the homeless man was a curiously exotic figure, outrageously Byronesque in a roll collar, flowing Windsor tie, cape, and oversized walking stick, Chicago's celebrated hobo, Ben Reitman. Perhaps more than any other individual in the United States, Ben Reitman understood the men who paced the streets of West Madison and other skid road haunts. The criminals and whores as well as the migrant workers confided in Ben Reitman.

Raised in a slum district in Chicago, Reitman had as a youngster learned the ways of the underclasses. He ran errands for prostitutes, ransacked trash cans and scrap piles for treasures to sell to junk men, and roamed the railroad yards for sport. He remembered seeing as a young boy many hoboes, hobo "Kings," and hunger marches. At age ten he clambered aboard an outbound freight heading east, took up with Ohio Skip and Cincinnati Slim, and became a fledgling hobo. Returning periodically to see his mother in Chicago, the youngster tramped across the country taking odd jobs and panhandling. He listened attentively to railroad chapel ministers and began to carry a Bible. He also began to attend night classes at the YMCA and to read voraciously. When the zeal for incessant tramping cooled temporarily, Reitman got a job at Chicago's Polyclinic Laboratory as a lab boy under the tutelage of Dr. Maximilian Herzog, a renowned pathologist and bacteriologist. Reitman kept at the job for several years and entered the College of Physicians and Surgeons as a medical student in 1900. He married in 1901, fathered a daughter, traveled to Europe, graduated from medical school in 1904, and divorced in 1905. At age twenty-five he opened a medical office on Chicago's South

Side and began to teach several courses at local colleges.

But the wanderlust had Reitman in a viselike grip. The
doctor would often shut down his office, head for the railroad yards, and jump a freight for places unknown. He explained his love of beating from town to town as a neuro-
pathic craziness, a fugue, "ambulatory automatism." It was
his hobby, his sport, and his disease. He served as a doctor to
a railroad section gang in Mexico, wandered through Europe, and saw the San Francisco earthquake in 1906. He also
met James Eads How in St. Louis, joined the International
Brotherhood Welfare Association, and, along with Irwin St.
John Tucker and others, opened the Chicago branch of the
Hobo College.

On January 23, 1907, the dark, strapping Reitman led a
parade of unemployed workers along the streets of Chicago.
Many unemployed heads were busted that day by overeager
Chicago police and the violence ignited a wave of stories, not
only in the public press but in radical sheets, about Ben
Reitman's involvement. The hobo physician had gained notoriety.

Soon after the unemployed workers' demonstration, the
anarchist Emma Goldman scheduled a speech in Chicago.
When the Chief of Police attempted to thwart Goldman's
friends from renting a hall, Reitman secretly offered the anarchists the Hobo College facilities. The offer was a fateful
gesture. Reitman and Emma Goldman became lovers and
fellow radicals. She wrote in her autobiography, "I had been
profoundly stirred by him. Our being much together since
had strengthened his physical appeal for me. I was aware
that he also had been aroused; he had shown it in every look,
and one day he had suddenly seized me in an effort to em-
brace me. I had resented his presumption, though his touch
had thrilled me. In the quiet of the night, alone with my
thoughts, I became aware of a growing passion for the wild-

looking handsome creature, whose hands exerted such fascination."

For ten years Reitman traveled with Emma Goldman,
distributing literature, arranging for lectures, writing and
speaking. During a San Diego free-speech fight, he was ab-
ducted by a local vigilante mob, stripped naked in the desert,
tarred, and, in the absence of feathers, sagebrushed. He was
arrested and jailed in New York and also Cleveland for dis-
seminating birth-control information.

Reitman's relationship with Emma Goldman gradually
cooled and she was later deported. Reitman married again in
1917 and resumed his medical practice, one which was dedicated to the care of prostitutes, pimps, criminals, and other
outcasts. Except for periodic tramping excursions, Reitman
was now settled as an eccentric Chicago celebrity.

Reitman more than once wrote that the early visit to St.
Louis and the meeting with James Eads How changed his
life and gave him vision and aspiration. "I saw new worlds to
conquer. I saw myself as the greatest of hoboes, the hobo
who would save all the rest of them from their homeless,
womanless, jobless lives."

When the hobo high priest opened the Big Chi branch of
the IBWA early in the century, it was not as a proselytizer
for the road but as an enemy of it. Reitman never recommended the hobo life to anyone. Indeed, he traveled the
country through the years telling young tramp boys that
they were headed for jail and ruin. At a lecture in New
York's Bowery Mission he told an audience of budding
tramps to go home. "How many of you are happy? What's
the use of going around like you are? Panhandling plays itself out. You can't be a tramp and stay out of the jug." One
boy, tears streaming from his face, broke in, "I thought it
would be fun to tramp, but it ain't." He went home the next
day.

In a remarkable, maundering composition jotted on the stationery of a St. Louis hotel, Reitman reveals the peculiar ambiguity of his feelings about a hobo existence. He both rhapsodizes on and assails the life of the road. He writes of the wanderlust clinically as if infection were brought on by some alien virus. Saint Paul had it; so did Lewis and Clark and Stanley and Livingston, hoboes all. No matter what city he has visited, no matter how long he has been on the road, the ravenous craving for motion is always there, a mania, a parching thirst, both a perverted delirium and an ecstasy. He knows no day when the yearning is not intense. He is tortured by it. Geneva, Glasgow, Hamburg, Naples, Havre—he has seen them all, beaten his way on railroads, steamships, eaten in Bowery missions, London soup kitchens, and at an Antwerp worker's home. And most of it was free. He remembers the deep grass of a Georgia field, the star-splashed skies of the Rockies, the smell of fresh hay of many a barn, the music of horses munching in their stalls. He quotes Kipling: "I've turned my 'and to most and turned it good."

Ben Reitman, although deadly serious about his efforts to improve the lot of the hobo, was a master showman. Often his antics appeared bizarre. It was a "hobo banquet" in the Windsor-Clifton Hotel on May 20, 1907, that gave Reitman national exposure. With reporters from national magazines and newspapers alerted to the bash, Reitman visited the Chicago House of Corrections, the county jail, the hospitals, lodges, missions, and barrelhouses looking for prospective guests. He found plenty. When he handed out invitations at Hinky Dink's saloon, he was almost mobbed.

Washington Flat, the planned toastmaster, didn't make the affair after being herded out of the city by police in the afternoon. The regular program began with a poem by Chicago Tommy entitled "The Face on the Barroom Floor," a rambling, morose tale about a hobo, Osler Joe, who had dropped dead in a saloon after dramatically drawing a picture of his lost angelic wife. Philadelphia Jack Brown also delivered a poem with sobering effect:

> When an old bum dies, bury him deep,
> Put a link at his head, put a pin at his feet;
> Put a solid draw-bar across his breast,
> For he is only an old-timer gone to his rest.

Although Reitman declared the banquet a success, he lamented that the reporters who covered the event saw only the hoopla and not the pathos. From the gutter bums to the boys who had only recently run away from home, the crowd could have told the writers a hundred poignant tales. But Reitman's serious purpose in gathering the men together was lost in stories the following day about hundreds of Weary Willies messing good hotel carpets.

In 1924, Reitman staged a coup that promised to dwarf all of his numerous attention-provoking spectaculars. The Grandview, a seventy-five-room hotel at 3801 Grand Boulevard, an infamous hangout for gamblers, pushers, and whores owned by the powerful South Side vice syndicate known as the Four Horsemen—Sol, Mike, Phil, and Abe— had fallen victim to one too many surprise visits by Chicago's finest. The Horsemen, deciding that discretion was the better part, uprooted the operation and moved on. As a gesture to friend Reitman, who had faithfully served as the hotel's physician to the prostitutes, they gave the hotel rent free for conversion into an establishment for the Doctor's homeless friends.

To Hogan's Flop and Muggsy's and the Hobo College, Reitman sent invitations to a grand opening for "God's Kingdom for Hoboes." A few days later a hundred of Ben's friends gathered on West Madison for a march to the "L" station at Wells Street and rode triumphantly on the cushions to the Kingdom. Reitman had bellboys for the occasion to assign and escort the guests to their rooms. Old Dad Spears, who hadn't slept in a real bed in years, drew room 203, the royal suite. He slept on the floor that night, not wanting to despoil the sheets.

The Kingdom thrived for one glorious month. As Reitman wrote later, with a bit of characteristic exaggeration, it was "not only a church and a university for many; it was the melting pot where hunger, poverty, misery and degradation of human lives were refined and transformed into ideals for a better and useful life." He especially remembered the Sunday afternoon concerts and community sings, hundreds joining in—hoboes, prostitutes, gamblers, even the policemen who were shadowing the Kingdom. A reporter from the *Tribune* remarked after attending one of the sings, "I've never heard such singing in my life. This is the most impressive service I've ever attended." Reitman agreed: "As the crowd sang it forgot that they were social outcasts. Song had united them into one great family. They sang for joy and were better for it. And the community was better for it."

The Kingdom's black neighbors thought otherwise—something about noise and unkempt people and plummeting property values caused by white trash. After the landlord successfully sued for possession, the Kingdom closed. But what a month it had been!

For many years the national as well as the Chicago press referred to Reitman as King of the Hoboes and Ben did little to discourage such an appellation. But Ben also accepted somewhat subordinate positions in the royal pecking order of hobo fraternal organizations. In 1933 King Jeff Davis, in his inimitable fashion, conferred upon Reitman and three others the Hoboes of America, Inc.'s highest order, below that of the lofty Davis himself, of course—the Order of

Knight of the Road. The Chicago *Daily News* reported, "Knighthood is in flower on the barren, sun-blistered, junk-strewn mesas which lie south of Van Buren street between Canal and Clinton streets." As cameramen from several newspapers, alerted to the open-air ceremony by the publicity-seeking Davis and the equally publicity-seeking Reitman, clicked away in amusement, four squires kneeled to begin the historic event. King Jeff sits on the oil-drum throne. He dubs knighthood on each of the squires. They deliver acceptance speeches. Sir Ben declares, "The good people of society were meeting and asking 'what shall we do for the hobo?' Now the hobo is meeting to discuss what he is going to do with society."

But Reitman's favor with King Jeff waxed and waned in the next few years as newspapers insisted on referring to Reitman as King of the Hoboes. And when Ben took no special pains to correct the writers, Davis, smelling treason and blasphemy, summoned the Hobo Doctor to a kangaroo court trial. Reitman was stripped of his knighthood and put on probation. His reaction: "There is nobody fit for the title but me, but I don't want it." Reitman had more important matters to attend to—the continuing activities of the Hobo College.

A CHICAGO INSTITUTION OF HIGHER LEARNING

When he was planning the structure of Chicago's Hobo College early in the century, Ben Reitman declared, "No ghost will be hovering to the background of the place. No sermons will be on the program. No 'woodyard' will be just around the corner ... and once a week we'll send one boy back home to mother; we'll settle ten hoboes a week to steady work who the day before had no work and settled place of existence farthest from their soberest thoughts; and, greater than these, we'll give to 10 percent—15—perhaps 20 percent of Chicago's 500 incoming wanderers daily a new, refreshing touch and reminder that they are still human in a world that has not lost all humanity." The College stationery called the institution a "service station, clearing house, and educational institute for homeless men. A laboratory for the study of unemployment and all other factors that tend to make men 'down and out.' "

For nearly three decades it worked. It certainly was no panacea for the ills of the homeless community and it didn't touch the number of lives that the ambitious Reitman had hoped, but the College did provide a valuable psychological and emotional outlet. It was part community center, part debating forum, part ego trip, part educational institution. Like the hobo community itself, it was unstructured, dynamic, and usually broke. And like the hobo community, it always seemed to be moving. In a chase with fire officials and unsympathetic merchant neighbors, the College changed Hobohemia locations almost yearly—133 S. Green, 1118 West Madison, 439 N. Clark, 913 W. Washington, 34 S. Peoria, 34 N. State, 641 W. Washington, 711 W. Harrison, 712 S. Halsted, and others. Although the locations varied, the appearance remained pretty much the same—a hall with a seating capacity of 150; shelves lined with volumes such as *Totemism and Exogamy* and *Darwin and After Darwin*, and magazines discarded by the Chicago Public Library; oil portraits of Voltaire, Erasmus, Darwin, Whitman, and Twain; a rusty stove where the cook, the "Bulgarian General," fried up a fine grade of horsemeat.

No bums were allowed to use the College facilities for cheap flops. The proprietors became so annoyed in the early days of the institution with the ne'er-do-wells falling asleep in the easy chairs during lectures that they held a ceremonial chair burning. In the place of the more luxurious furnishings appeared austere, backless benches appropriate only for sober, attentive hobo students and not for social pests. The benches were dubbed "anti-booze, anti-snooze, church pews."

The faculty included Professor Paddy Corrall, who taught "How to live without eating"; Professor John Laughman on street speaking; Professor Nels Anderson of the University of Chicago on the history of vagrancy; E. W. Burgess of the University of Chicago on sociology; David Rotman on psychiatry; Frank Beck on social pathology; the author Jim Tully on the philosophy of the road; and Professor Ohio Skip on geography (best towns to hit and miss and the habits of bulls and bulldogs in each). Perhaps the most engaging of all courses in the curriculum was "Stalking the bummee, proper approach, facial expression, and how to throw the feet," something of a finishing-school seminar. Suggestions and addenda on this subject could surge forth from all parts of a filled hall at any time.

Resident scholars included Statistical Slim Brundage, a walking encyclopedia of tariff rates and population figures; Billy Whiskers, the red-nosed Santa Claus; and Jack Macbeth, whom many considered the ultimate egghead. "At the moment," he once declared, "I am mostly concerned with astronomy, prehistoric man and psychology of the nonconformist group." The deacon of visiting soapbox orators at the College was one "Professor Budman," a long-time dean of the world of 'boes, who held audiences spellbound not only in Chicago but on main stems all across the land. His topic: the necessity for instituting a one-hour work day, one-day work week.

Sir Knight Pat Salmon gave numerous lectures on the subject of leisure. Warning that untrained idlers, such as kids just out of school, were in danger of becoming society's

lotus eaters, Pat held up the hobo as the true leisure philosopher. Quoting Wordsworth, Longfellow, and Cowper, he
called the hobo a stern realist, always on his toes, noble in
his workless hours, practical, a thinker ready to spring
against all obstacles presented by man and nature, a survivor
of the fittest. And then there was the poet laureate, A. W.
Dragstedt. One of his compositions delivered at the College:

> *I had a dream some time ago*
> *Like only those can have*
> *Whose learning goes for higher dope*
> *And pure scientific salve.*
>
> *The judges of the great world court*
> *Made laws to change all breeds,*
> *So Chinamen can angels be*
> *And Negroes can be Swedes.*
>
> *No longer men can heroes be*
> *When shot with bullets full,*
> *For guns and cannons are but used*
> *For shooting of the bull.*

The College at times sent visiting lecturers to the University of Chicago's sociology department to address students
and faculty on subjects of mutual interest. Mike Smith of
New York, "Chinatown Whitie," fascinated his audiences
with discourses on unemployment among migratory workers; Frank Gibbons of Chicago, "Chicago Red," gave ento-
mological perorations on the habits of insects in lodging
houses from New York to California.

A typical night at the College: Superintendent John
Laughman, Irish, college educated, a superior orator, opens
the meeting by introducing a Professor Davis who lectures
on the subject "Successful Panhandling." Director Reitman,
dressed in a shabby gray suit, enters and makes a plea for do-
nations to keep the College operating. Laughman passes the

dishpan while Reitman pleads for quarters and dimes. One wag remarks, "The Irishman takes up the money but the Jew gets it." Ben, who often panhandled tickets to operas and shows for the men, announces that fifty seats to the Harris Theater are available for the asking. After the fund raising, the hobo students are free to question the speaker and give talks or tirades of their own. One student pushes for the single tax; another pushes against the World Court. The speechmaking concluded, the audience hears a rendition of "The Portland County Jail" performed by a very drunk Jimmy, the Caruso of Hobo College. Laughman concludes the evening with a recitation of the needs of the hobo. Out in the lobby the soloist attempts to panhandle the other visitors.

Some University of Chicago students frequented the halls of Hobo College for reciprocal doses of extra curricular erudition. The student exchanges once led to a formal debate between a team of hoboes—Boxcar Bennie, Larry the Loud, and Fred Fourdice—and the University's debating team. The semicloistered lads from academe were in over their heads. After an embarrassing drubbing by the road veterans—masters of elocution, deduction, evasion, and quick wit all—one of the university team members remarked about the victors, "They are really good speakers . . . many of the men are college graduates; one I know is a graduate of Oxford University." A study by Northwestern psychology students on the intellectual capabilities of Hobo College students would not have surprised the University of Chicago debating team. Eighty hoboes at the College agreed to take the army Alpha intelligence tests. The results, obviously an unscientific barometer but nevertheless revealing, found the 'boes intellectually superior to average university seniors.

The College promoted the arts. President Irwin St. John Tucker and Director Reitman once landed opera star Mary

Garden for a guest appearance on the College stage. To a building bulging with hoboes, Garden gave such a stirring performance that the audience erupted during the finale with aggressive foot stomping. Tucker anxiously asked the men to clap instead. Although the ancient structure housing the College had survived the Great Fire, it seemed on the verge of collapse. As Garden left the stage, a hobo graybeard took the star's hand and eloquently remarked, "By the eternal gods—Per deus eternus—eterni—etern—you're a damn good singer." Garden was overwhelmed. "That's the finest compliment I've had this season. I'm coming to sing for you again next year."

Graduation day, 1926, was typical of many held by the College through the years. There were speeches, a musical concert, and the baccalaureate address by Professor E. L. Shaub, Professor of Philosophy at Northwestern. Ben Reitman passed out the diplomas which read:

> BE IT KNOWN TO ALL THE WORLD THAT———has been a student at THE HOBO COLLEGE and has attended the lectures, discussions, clinics, musicals, readings, and visits to art galleries and theaters.
>
> He has also expressed a desire to get an education, better his own conditions and help build a world that will be without unemployment, poverty, wars, prostitution, ignorance, and injustice.
>
> He pledges himself to try individually to live a clean, honest, manly life, and to take care of his health and morals, and abstain from all habits that undermine his health and better nature. He agrees to cooperate with all people and organizations that are really trying to abolish poverty and misery, and to work to build a better world in which to live.

One visitor who witnessed the event later wrote, "After Prof. Shaub's lecture was a time to say 'good-bye.' Some of these men would never see the Hobo College again—who could tell what would happen to them by the time the Hobo

College opened its doors next winter. Many of the old broken derelicts wept—this had been the one anchor in their lives for many a year."

The fraternal ceremonies, debates, readings, and sings at the College were a welcome relief to numerous weary men of the road who passed through its doors. But much of the activity was misunderstood by the public and newspaper and magazine writers who failed to see the earnest purpose behind the College's existence. Much of the ceremony was self-parody; much of the humor had a gallows flavor; much of the public activity, although surrounded in ludicrous pomp, carried a message. But the press continued to treat the College as a comic travesty. After one particularly annoying piece of burlesque in the Chicago *Herald*, Michael C. Walsh, one of the College's directors, wrote the editor that "migratory workers are victims of the most damnable outrages which any members of the human race must endure. When the free-born American citizen seeks employment in Louisiana, Alabama, Arkansas, Mississippi, Texas, and Kansas he is sentenced to eleven months and twenty days' hard labor in the convict camps for the crime of asking for work. He is forced to labor beneath the whip at building roads, hewing lumber and boiling turpentine. He attends a college in which the sheriff is chief instructor and with vicious men as assistant professors. They do their instructing with rifles as text books. . . . We seek to teach these men the elements of law and to provide them with the means whereby they can protect themselves. Funny, isn't it? . . . Great joke, isn't it?"

After the College had been in Hobohemia for nearly two decades, Ben Reitman looked back: "Thousands of men have stopped a little while with us and have been brought in contact with philosophy and psychology, with art and letters and music." An oasis in a homeless man's desert of despair.

NELS ANDERSON

From the first part of the century, Chicago's homeless desert had been scrutinized by sociologists, criminologists, psychologists, and numerous other writers, amateur and professional. The lonely wanderers of the main stem and its branches had been counted, interviewed, followed, infiltrated, categorized, and analyzed. But in 1923 the University of Chicago Press published the most far-reaching examination of Hobohemia ever undertaken, *The Hobo: The Sociology of the Homeless Man.* It was written by Nels Anderson.

Son of an immigrant hobo Swede, Anderson spent his early years selling newspapers along West Madison and then hit the road as a skinner, working the harvests and mines, and as a bridge snake, a structural-iron itinerant. Traveling across the continent, with intermittent stops in Chicago, he eventually took up with a Mormon family in Utah, converted to the religion, and attended college at Brigham Young University. After a stint overseas in the army, Anderson ended up back in Chicago as a graduate student in sociology at the University of Chicago. After he had been at the University for a few months, the hobo-turned-student heard Ben Reitman lecture on social work. Always trying to stimulate debate, Reitman began taunting the social workers in the audience, asserting that their efficiency training tended to make them cold and impersonal in relations with the poor. The one in the crowd who rose to challenge that charge most vigorously was Nels Anderson. A half-hour exchange between the two resulted in a Reitman invitation to retire to a coffee shop for further discussion. Reitman began to talk of the need of a penetrating study of the homeless men in Chicago—who they were, why they gathered there, and how they survived or didn't survive. At a subsequent meeting, the hobo physician announced to Anderson that Dr. William Evans, longtime head of Chicago's Public Health Department and close personal friend of Reitman, had agreed to pledge enough money for Anderson to begin the study.

Along the curbs, in the lodging houses and outside the cat houses, in the parks and museums, at the lake-front jungles, Anderson sought out the drifters and loners and tried to piece together the puzzles of the stem. Because of his own wanderings and close association with working stiffs and alkis, Anderson was able, as no one before, to detail the personalities and dynamics of life in Hobohemia. The book received nationwide interest and acclaim. Harry Kemp, for example, applauded the effort to treat the hobo and tramp community with understanding and social perspective.

But not everyone was happy with the work. The *Hobo World*, ignorant of Anderson's experiences on the road, called the book another half-baked academic treatise by one who had not blistered his hands on a rattler or tasted the life of the jungle. Although the attack by the hobo newspaper was essentially an attack against a writer it didn't consider one of the fraternity, the review did make one good point. The book was primarily a study of skid road and the social flotsam of Chicago's inner city and not of the life of the American hobo outside of Chi. Anderson's title for the book was somewhat misleading.

And years later Anderson himself looked back on his work on the hobo community and pointed out another weakness of his study—an important oversight. He remembered strolling along West Madison with Jacob Coxey, the general of the 1893 march on Washington. Coxey had casually predicted, "The old-timers will not be here much longer." The General had been speaking of the traditional hobo, the migrant worker who came to Chicago because it was the transportation center for his kind, the employment center, the information and entertainment and intellectual center. As the West was filling with permanent residents, as mining and lumber camps became mining and lumber towns with their own reservoirs of laborers, as machines replaced men in the harvest fields and need for hobo labor declined, the glory days of West Madison, the era of Hobohemia in Chicago, would soon be drawing to a close. Although he didn't see the pattern in the twenties, it was there, and Anderson wrote later, "It is clear now, although it was not recognized fully at the time, that the hobo was on his way out."

A MECCA NO MORE

At the time of Nels Anderson's study in 1923, the market demand for hobo labor was diminishing. As the population increased in towns and cities of the West, work in the mines and harvest fields and orchards was increasingly filled by locals, "home guards," who took odd jobs much as the hobo but preferred to stay close to home. Many migrant workers now rode in automobiles or pulled trailers. West Madison Street was not part of their lives. And by the thirties and the Great Depression, public and private relief agencies had absorbed many of the relatively helpless vagrants who would have been on the road or in the West Madison gutters years before. Hospitals, insane asylums, CC camps, and transient shelters now housed many of the feebleminded, epileptic, tubercular, and elderly. And although the road was alive as never before with Okies and Arkies rolling dying tin lizzies across the West and with other men, women, and children seeking salvation on the freights heading to places unknown, West Madison Street was not part of their lives either. In the early 1920s the Desplaines Street Police Station had housed from fifty to a hundred men on cold nights. In 1939 it was housing none. The Desplaines Station sergeant was somewhat surprised at the lack of hobo and other homeless guests: "We don't know why it is that no one comes to the station anymore, all the hoboes seem to be taken care of at the shelter houses, missions, or are able to provide for themselves." Few of the typical hoboes the sergeant had known in the twenties were on the stem, because the railroad hobo, as the sergeant had known him, was a dying species.

As the numbers of traditional hoboes dwindled on the streets of the West Madison area, many of the old-time legends also began to disappear. In 1934 Hobohemia lost one of its most colorful figures, Harry Batter, radical orator of Bughouse Square. Seventy-five mourners sang the old IWW marching song "Hallelujah I'm a Bum!" at Harry's wake and listened to the Hobo's Prayer:

> ALMIGHTY GOD, heavenly father who has blessed us hobos with good health and avid appetites and made this world a bountiful and plentiful place for all of us bipeds with towering possibilities: Give us common sense enough to wander and roam the world, and make the freights easier to get and the chickens to come closer to the jungles that we hobos might have chicken-stew oftener. Abolish, O Lord, the lousy flophouses and ungodly vagrancy laws and their concomitants, the rock-piles. Send us, O Lord, more sunshine and less winter, so we can enjoy our leisure time more, and grant us the privilege to ride the cushions gratis. For these simple and elemental things we will forever praise thee, O Lord! Amen.

Harry's estate was divided among the mourners—twenty-five cents each. Harry had lit his stove with what he thought was kerosene. It was gasoline. They spread Harry's ashes over the graves of the Haymarket anarchist martyrs buried in Waldheim Cemetery.

Harry Batter's demise seemed to trigger an ominous spate of deaths among Chicago's hobo community in the next few

years. In 1936 Mother Greenstein was also buried at Waldheim. At the annual Christmas banquet, which Mother
Greenstein had been planning, Ben Reitman took her place
at the head table and declared, "She was a great soul. The
hoboes didn't have to believe in Santa Claus; they believed
in Mother Greenstein." A poem among the personal papers
left by Ben Reitman talked of his close friend:

> *You gave your life, your every day,*
> *To help the poor, the weak astray.*
> *To build a world that only you*
> *Had faith it some day will come true.*
> *A world where poverty and pain*
> *Will not be used to power gain*
> *By cruel drones whose minds are set*
> *On gilded thrones of war and death,*
> *A world where all shall live in peace,*
> *Where all shall strive to others please,*
> *A life, you Mother Greenstein gave*
> *Your work, that we this life may live.*

The next year Red Martha Biegler passed away. Martha
had operated a free boarding house at 357 W. Chicago Avenue. Among her boarders had been Boxcar Bertha Thomp-
son, whose autobiography Ben Reitman had edited for publication. Just as Mother Greenstein had never denied a bite
to eat to a hungry man, Red Martha, many 'boes testified,
had never refused a cold man a free flop.

That same year another crusty radical hobo, old Dad
Crouch, departed the main stem for good. Ben Reitman pre-
sided over the services and reminded the mourners of Dad's
performance at one of the Hobo College's debates with the
University of Chicago debating team. The topic for discussion: Should all men strive for a college education? Arguing
the affirmative, of course, were the eager college boys. Arguing the negative, with passion, were Old Dad and his col-
leagues. The subject had offended Dad, a gnarled, crippled

veteran of the road and the soapbox, and he hurled invective, sarcasm, wit, and icy epithets at the intimidated opposition. They cowered in ignominious defeat.

Not only legendary figures were dying in Hobohemia; sacred institutions were passing on. For sixteen years the Dill Pickle Club at 18 Tooker Place had served as a bastion of offbeats, a nest for radicals of all stripes. They had discussed the great issues of the moment at the Dill, from prohibition to the Al Capone defense fund. All types and kinds had flocked there—Clarence Darrow, Sherwood Anderson, Carl Sandburg, Emma Goldman, bohemian poets, labor leaders, free-lovers, Spanish spiritualists, critics, Yellow Kid Weil, the high financier, anybody and everybody anxious to express and expose themselves to their fellow travelers and to the next morning's newspaper readers. The Internal Revenue Service delivered the guillotine blow, cutting off the club for nonpayment of taxes. The *Chicago Herald and Examiner* lamented, "Goodbye, Dill Pickle. Of all the 57 varieties, you were the most entertaining."

Ben Reitman died in 1942. He played the showman to the end. The doctor stipulated in his will that "two hundred and fifty dollars shall be spent for food and drink for Hoboes and unemployed who will be invited by my son to a funeral dinner. I should like the service to be in a big hall, with drink, fun, and a happy good time for all."

Frank Beck, friend and associate of Ben Reitman, once called West Madison the "port of missing men." Thousands of drifters and working stiffs passed through West Madison in the live years and were fed, boarded, clothed, entertained, conned, shipped out, treated, enriched, and devastated. But those were the live years. By 1942, West Madison was just another dirty skid-road street.

8/ "In the Sunset of Hobo Oblivion"

BILL QUIRKE, the well-known writer and poet for the *Hobo News*, wrote in 1921 about large numbers of men and women in cars working as fruit glommers in the Northwest, ousting many hobo stiffs from their jobs. Mostly stump ranchers and home-guard workers from nearby towns, the car-borne pickers could move from job to job more quickly than the train jumpers, were willing to work for cheaper wages because many had extra family members along who added to the income, and had fewer political leanings than the regular stiffs, many of whom were veterans of Wobbly wars. At a packinghouse in Yakima, Washington, the foreman of a hop ranch told Quirke that he and other foremen in the area had orders not to take on floater workers, only home guards.

Arizona Bob Gillespie, an old desert rat who worked with Jeff Davis in the Hoboes of America, Inc., remarked that times had changed in the West. The concrete roads, Bob said, had spawned thousands of rubber tramps who traveled in ancient cars and replaced hobo labor in the berry fields. The day of the authentic, train-jumping, jungling hobo, he said, was on its way out.

The era of the hobo had grown with the railroad and the rapidly expanding industries to which it brought life. But with increased mechanization in the major industries that traditionally hired seasonal and casual labor—farming, logging, mining, and construction—the hobo found his economic world crumbling. As combines and other machines appeared in the fields, the prairie farmers, for example, needed fewer and fewer hobo workers. Just as improved technology had outmoded jobs in the industrial East, machines were now taking on much of the field labor in the Grain Belt.

At the same time technology was making hobo labor increasingly superfluous, the rubber-tramp workers that Bill Quirke and Arizona Bob talked about were giving the old-time hoboes tough competition. As the formerly isolated sodbusters in the trans-Mississippi West were joined by a swelling cadre of other settlers, as desolate frontier settlements became growing towns, the West now had a sprouting source of local labor, much of it made mobile by the automobile. No longer did farmers have to rely on the annual horde of migratory blackbirds; no longer was the muscle of hobo labor as indispensable to the prairie as it once had been. In his book *Men on the Move*, published in 1940, Nels Anderson saw the hobo of the twenties as a dying breed. The nomadic train jumpers, he wrote, were becoming in these years economic debris. Reflecting on Anderson's book, Ben Reitman wrote, "The dreaming, wandering Willie that Anderson described in his 'milk and Honey Route' has disappeared, as has Walt Whitman's hero of the 'Open Road,' and the 1920 hobo, vagrant, and tramp has become the 1940 migrant, transient, and refugee."

Refugees—the Great Depression made them by the thousands. If the twenties had witnessed the erosion of the traditional hobo life on the road, the Depression thirties brought even more disruption. When the protean wanderers of earlier times, the hoboes, had foraged the country in search of work, they had usually found it, however grueling; they formed part of an economic system and filled an important industrial role. When the thousands hit the freights and highways in the thirties, they found few jobs on the road. John Dos Passos told of seeing unemployed wanderers in Detroit living in caves dug out of sand piles. Similar scenes

across the country were commonplace: Okie and Arkie families rolling across the West, their lives drying up like the
prairie dust they left behind; tough, calloused factory workers hustling for odd jobs and even peddling doughnuts and
apples in city slums; broke businessmen joining the freight-
hoppers and soup-liners they had, in better times, flippantly
scorned as lazy parasites; jobless fathers on the road joining
old-time hoboes in the Sallies and the missions. These were
not the migratory workers of earlier years but refugees, dis-
possessed, the palsied victims of economic disease.

In these battalions of jobless and homeless were thousands
of boys and girls, many under fifteen; with the security of
their homes breaking apart, they hit the freights and highways in droves. *Fortune* magazine in February 1933 estimated that 200,000 young men and boys, many suffering
from disease and malnutrition, were aimlessly drifting by
freight across the country. Thomas Minehan of the University of Minnesota, who interviewed hundreds of these road
kids in the early thirties, wrote of mobs of children on the
trains, including many girls "dressed in overalls or Army
breeches and boys' coats or sweaters—looking, except for
their dirt and rags, like a Girl Scout club on an outing."
Lowell Norris, in an article in *Scribner's Magazine* in May
1933, concluded that the traditional hobo was not found in
these ranks. "Very few of them could be classified as habitual vagrants," he wrote, "almost none could be said to belong to the criminal classes." In the New York subway,
twelve- and thirteen-year-old boys grappled for scraps from
trash cans. In city after city, sick teenagers lined up in soup
lines and flopped in municipal lodging houses already bulging with the destitute. Kids froze to death in city slums;
others starved. This was the human dross of the Depression,
the most horrifying manifestation of economic plague.

The road voices of the thirties were mournful and haunting, dirgelike testimonies of hopelessness and fatigued spirit: "As I looked at these unfortunates sprawled on the cement floors, scratching the vermin that clung to their unwashed bodies, I thought to myself what patience Americans have, to bear with scarcely a murmur an existence unfit for a dog." "One place is about as good as another for a man on the bum. I'll hold the town down as long as I can and then shove off to somewhere else." "Men like us aren't human beings. We're criminals, just like rats, hunting for food and shelter."

The Great Depression filled two-bit flophouses and missions of the skid roads and made canned heaters and gutter bums of workers and businessmen alike. But if the Starvation Army that filled the freights and flophouses in the thirties still had some seasoned migrants, bughouse philosophers, and old Wobs, it now had whole families frantically on the move. In some of the small towns along the railroad lines, the population doubled or tripled instantly with the arrival of a train—kids, women, boomers, crooks, enough of a cross-section of Americana to keep a sociologist in subjects for a long time. One 'bo, looking back on these days, wrote, "On a single westbound drag I counted females by the score: old women, young women, girls in couples or unattached, children traveling with their families, dames riding alone or with their husbands or chance acquaintances." It was as if the whole country were in motion, on foot, in cars, on the rails, trying to stave off ultimate disaster by running.

And the horror on the road was unrelieved, incomprehensible, mirrored in a sea of blank, bewildered faces. One of the rail riders interviewed by Studs Terkel told of a baby smothering to death in her mother's arms in a smoke- and soot-choked railroad tunnel; one remembered fresh corpses floating in the Detroit river, poverty-wracked people who had traded in their poverty; another recalled families living in huts made from fruit boxes. And along the highways moved the Dust Bowl refugees riveted so powerfully on the public consciousness by the songs of Woody Guthrie: the thousands displaced by the insidious blanket of black, their earthly belongings piled in rickety tin lizzies, herded, hounded, and hunted by police and vigilantes, drifting like the dust from which they ran, the Tom Joads leading their battered families on a "never-ending highway" toward the mythical promised land of jobs and honest pay and finding, instead, injustice and intolerance.

Blacks, as usual, made out worse than the whites on the road. The Depression was only a further extension of their own perpetual depression. Louis Banks had left his Arkansas cotton-farm home for the road. He told Terkel of the hard times: of losing a job because of his race while two white buddies were hired; of a couple of train dicks shooting everything that moved; of sleeping with black alkies in Los Angeles who had only newspapers to ward off the night cold; of working as a chef for half the money made by whites.

R. D. Ginther, a Wobbly and cook and for many years an official of the Seattle Cooks and Waiters Union, began in the mid-thirties to capture in crude, India-ink and watercolor paintings the horror of the Depression and the men whose lives ended in skid road. Working in his basement, sometimes dead drunk, Ginther painted angry scenes of a dehumanized, berserk world of drunks and thieves, tomato-can vags and snowbirds. These were skeletal phantoms, their faces cracked and cold and, like their lives, decayed. Here are decrepit bums puking on dehorned alcohol; men with freshly slit wrists; wasted souls along curbs; lineups in city jails—figures abject and debased. Absent is the notion of vagabond freedom and individualism. Gone are the days of the working men of the road and the Wobbly vision of the One Big Union. For Ginther, it had all ended here in the filth and scum and hell of flophouses, missions, and alleys. In only one painting does a familiar hobo scene penetrate Ginther's images of the Depression. Several hoboes are camped outside Seattle preparing mulligan, gathering wood, reading their shirts for lice. Although the figures are grim, here at least are woods and companionship, relief from the hollow cold of city steel and concrete. But this painting was an aberration among the large number that came up from R. D. Ginther's basement, a memory of earlier times. In Ginther's world the hobo and Wobbly ideal had been perverted into the horror of the Depression gutter.

As the Depression drove thousands to the road in the thirties, it did not, many 'boes attested, resurrect the traditional hobo life. Instead, the thirties only made the lot of the old-time hobo more difficult. Some of the new road nomads eventually found relief in the CCC, the WPA, and other federal programs; others continued to haunt the soup kitchens and the missions. But for the hobo, the life was never the same. The glory days of the boomer workers, the knights of the tie and rail, had been eclipsed. As Ben Benson, the old hobo spokesman, declared in the forties, "If this was the beginning of the century I was talking to you boys: I would advise you all to 'hit the road.' For many men and boys who had the right stuff—sometimes called the American Rugged Individualism—made good. But, I regret to say, 'them days are gone forever!' "

"NEVER GONNA CEASE"

I had to take on whatever Mother Nature threw at me as her most ardent pupil and disciple and bona fide American hobo, what's left of us as we walk in the sunset of Hobo oblivion.

—Lord Open Road, Britt Convention

It is late in Britt. Around a low-dancing fire and simmering mulligan, a dozen or so 'boes are clapping and stomping as Rattlesnake Dick picks vigorously an old hobo ditty. Between the tunes, the men reel off their stories of the road, of holding down dicers and rattlers, of mean bulls and hostile towns, the frenzied running from state to state and city to city, of outwitting shacks, days in jails, and all the jobs, the places, and the fellow stiffs that made up their lives on the road. It is an atavistic ritual, this scene around the campfire, a nostalgic longing to recapture the tribal spirit. To a few, to Steam Train Maury, Mountain Dew, Virginia Slim, Hobo Adam Ydobon (*nobody* spelled backward), Portland Gray, and others, the road is still challenge, still represents freedom and defiance, is still the only life. But the hobo experience, they admit, is now mostly story and legend. Like the old freights which stand idle and abandoned along weed-choked railroad sidings, the hobo is an anachronism. But that does not stop these men from carrying on the life. Mountain Dew says the hobo experience has much to teach a modern America strapped to daily routine. The Cheyenne Kid insists that many Americans still crave the independence of movement represented by the hobo. "They're envious," he says, "they'd like to break away and do the same thing themselves." One of the 'boes quipped, however, that most people couldn't be hoboes if you "gave them a road map." But if the hobo has gone the way of the Santa Fe trail driver and the buffalo hunter, the idea of the hobo is still compelling. The dreamer, iconoclast, pioneer, he pricks the yearning to break new ground, to be at the cutting edge of a frontier, to explore. William Metzler, an agricultural economist, remarked a few years ago that the workers of the road were the "last free folk we have." The antithesis to an organized and regimented society, the hobo refuses a niche in the ordered world. "His future may be guaranteed for the rest of his life," Metzler said, "but he doesn't want to get up every morning in that same confounded little house and go through that confounded routine every day."

But as the years go by, it's getting tougher and tougher to live on the road, the surviving 'boes grimly explain. Not only did the increased industrialization and the successful taming and filling up of the virgin lands in the West render hobo labor unnecessary, the mechanization of the railroad seriously impaired the traditional mode of travel. In 1946, Jeff Davis told a reporter in Chicago that modernization of the railroads would be the final blow to the hobo. Ten years later he declared his prophecy a fact. "The 'boes are all settled down now, like me," the seventy-two-year-old, domesticated King concluded at a birthday party in Tonawanda, New York. "Tonawanda's a big rail junction where some of the roughest hobo camps used to be," said Jeff, "but now all the 'boes there are working for Wurlitzer, making jukeboxes."

Sparky Smith laments that the chalked signs have disappeared with the rest of the trappings of the life. "It's getting rougher every year," he says. "Along the railroad tracks there used to be markings about where you could get a handout. Them markings are all gone now."

Frying Pan Jack, with fifty-two years of the road and countless short-term jobs as a gandy and farm worker behind him, is now on Social Security and an army pension. His ruddy face framed by a wispy, white beard and wire spectacles, Jack seems younger than a man of sixty-five. Life on the freights has sustained him. "Me retire? How could I be an old man who sits up in a house and watches TV? I know that any town I've ever been into, I can go back and get a welcome. People will say 'Hello, Jack, glad to see you.' " That, he says, is the most beautiful gift he can get.

But the life has changed drastically and nowhere is that more evident than the trains themselves. "Higher wheels, so it's harder to get on a freight. Fewer boxcars, everything's going to be piggyback." Today, he notes, the trains go 250 miles without stopping. In the old days the trains would often stop every twenty-five miles at water tanks or coal chutes. They used to be seventy-five cars or less. "Now they're 200 to 250 cars. Can't even see the middle of the train."

Jeff Davis had said in the forties that the mechanization of the railroad was the final harbinger of the hobo demise. An incident at the Buffalo railroad yard in 1938 illustrates what he meant. An engineer, fireman, and conductor of the Twentieth Century Limited, together with two policemen, worked for half an hour extracting a befuddled hobo from behind the tender of the new streamlined train. The embarrassed stiff had gotten stuck in the new-style coupling hose. The American hobo had faced starvation, ridicule, jails, tough bulls, bad weather, bad jobs, and bad flops, but these new machines were another matter.

As a young boy, William O. Douglas had worked the packing houses, orchards, and harvests of Washington State, had roamed with hard-travelin' drifters and Wobbly organizers on the freights; shared stew and stories with vagabonds under railroad bridges and in work camps; known the fear and despair, the warmth and compassion of migrant workers. He wrote in his autobiography that he found more idealism and kindness from the people under those bridges and in the camps than from sanctimonious church elders and bank presidents who professed Christian love and charity and made their money riding the backs of the poor. Before his death, Justice Douglas, one of the Supreme Court's most fierce defenders of personal liberty, wrote out funeral instructions. He asked that the Woody Guthrie song "This Land Is Your land" be sung at the services and that the choice be explained. The song, he said, was not a "socialist dream of mind" but Guthrie's way of expressing what Douglas considered a constitutional right to wander freely across America, the right to be a drifter and vagabond. In February 1972, Douglas delivered an opinion in a case involving eight defendants convicted of violating a Jacksonville, Florida, vagrancy ordinance, a law which included under its sanctions all persons "wandering or strolling around from place to place without any lawful purpose or object." Invoking Walt Whitman's "Song of the Open Road" and Vachel Lindsay's "I Want to Go Wandering," Douglas argued that such spirit of independence must not be stifled, that the amenities of wandering freely "have dignified the right of dissent and have honored the right to be nonconformists and the right to defy submissiveness." Such amenities have, Douglas continued, "encouraged lives of high spirits rather than hushed, suffocating silence."

As Virginia Slim said before leaving Britt, "America's still a free country and a man if he chooses to may lead a lifestyle that he pursues as long as he doesn't harm his fellow man." The words sound much like those of William Douglas.

Ben Benson had said that the days were gone forever. But as Lord Open Road and Portland Gray get ready to head for the lonely tracks outside of Britt; as the newly elected King of the Hoboes, Steam Train Maury Graham, makes plans to visit more schools and veterans homes; as the surviving hobo guitar pickers strum new tunes and compose new rhymes, the call of the road seems alluring still. For these men, anyway, old Ben's peroration on the end of the American hobo is somewhat premature.

And so they continue their wandering, beating across the

country as so many in the hobo culture did before them, driven by the need to be different, to be, as Robert Service put it, a "race of men that don't fit in." For these men the old hobo song still rings true: "It looks like I'm never gonna cease my wanderin'."

A Glossary of the Road

The argot of the road evolved with the mingling of railroad workers, boomers, hoboes, tramps, and criminals in the cities, in jungles, on freights, in the railroad yards, in jails. The following glossary is not intended to be exhaustive but merely suggestive of the kind of language shared by many on the road. The terms and definitions were gathered from hoboes and various writers who used and heard the language through the years. Although some of the language changed with time and some terms varied in meaning from one part of the country to another, many of the words remained fairly constant. The following list attempts only to give those that were most widely used.

Alki. Alcohol; an alcoholic.

Angel food. Mission sermon.

Antique. Old-timer on the road.

Balloon. Pack or bedroll.

Batter. To beg.

Benny. Overcoat.

Bindle stiff. Hobo who carries a bundle, usually containing shirts, socks, razor, etc.

Blanket stiff. Hobo who carries a blanket and other personal possessions; used mostly on Pacific Coast.

Block scrapings. Meat begged from a butcher.

Blowed-in-the-glass stiff. Upper crust of the professional tramp class.

Blowing smoke. Boasting.

Boil up. To wash clothes and at the same time kill vermin that infest them.

Bone polisher. Wicked dog.

Boomer. Seasonal or migratory worker.

Booze hoister. Heavy drinker.

Bridge snake. Structural iron worker who usually carried hand tools for work on bridges, culverts, fences, etc.

Bull. Detective or any officer of the law.

Bull cook. Camp flunkey.

Bull horrors. Obsessive fear of police.

Buzz. To beg.

C. and A. pockets. Huge pockets on the inside of a coat for carrying food; named for the Chicago and Alton Railroad, the "Carry-All," which was most inhospitable to hoboes.

Calling in, catting in. Using another's campfire to cook.

Cally. Police station.

Canned heater. One who drank a deadly potion of cheap alcohol and water.

Carry the banner. To walk the streets all night.

Checkerboard crew. Mixed crew of white and black workers.

Chuck-a-dummy. To fake a fainting fit in order to get sympathy.

Cinder dick. Railway policeman.

Clover kicker. Farmer.

Cowcatcher. A slanted frame on the front of an engine to throw off cattle and other obstructions.

Croaker, crocus. Doctor.

Crumb boss. Janitor or porter for Western construction-camp bunkhouses.

Crumbs. Lice.

Crummy. Caboose; in early days of the boomer railroader, cabooses were often plagued with lice.

Death woods. Plank above the coupling of boxcars.

Deep-sea chef. Dishwasher.

Dehorn. Denatured alcohol.

Dicer. Fast freight.

Dick. Detective.

Dimmer. Dime.

Dingbat. Professional itinerant tramp beggar.

Dip. Pickpocket.

Ditch. To put off a train.

Doughhead. Baker.

Drag. Slow freight.

Drag, on the. On the road.

Drill. To walk or hike.

Flip. To hop a train

Flop. Place to sleep.

Fly mugs. Private police.

Frisk a drag. To search a freight for a suitable riding place.

Fuzzy tail. Tramp in bad humor.

Galway. Priest; name of county in Ireland applied to Irish-Catholic priests.

Gandy dancer. Hobo shovel stiff; track section hand.

Gas. Wood alcohol; doped cider; ether.

Gat. Gun.

Gay cat. Usually refers to amateur or tenderfoot hobo; sometimes used to describe lower-class stiffs.

Gila-monster route. Part of Southern Pacific running through Maricopa County, Ariz., to Yuma; many 'boes were ditched in Gila Bend, a desert town on that route.

Gink. Poor unfortunate.

Glims. Spectacles.

Going on the farm. Going on a side track.

Gondola. Flat freight car with no top.

Gooseberrying. Stealing clothes off a clothesline.

Graveyard. Hash.

Gump. Chicken.

Gunsel, guntzel. Green youth.

Guts. Meat, usually sausage.

Harness bulls. Uniformed police.

Hay bag. Woman on the road.

Headlights. Eggs.

High fence. Man's white neck collar.

Hiker. Town marshal.

His nibs. Police court judge.

Hitting the grit. Hiking or walking on foot along tracks.

Hog. Locomotive.

Home guard. Native; nonmigrating worker.

Hoop chisler. Peddler of worthless rings and watches.

Horstile, hostile. Used to describe towns unfriendly to hoboes.

Hot shot. Fast freight.

Hump. Mountain.

Iron man. Silver dollar.

Jackrolling. Robbing a drunk or other stiff.

Jerries. Section hands.

Jiggers. Pretended affection; used to elicit sympathy while begging.

Jim Hill wagon. Train of the Great Northern Railroad built by railroad mogul James J. Hill.

Jocker. Road kid's teacher and companion.

John Hollow Legs. Hungry stiff.

Johnny O'Brien. Boxcar.

Johnson Family. Used to describe yegg community.

Join out. To hire out in order to gain transportation.

Jolt. Penitentiary sentence.

Juble joo. Yegg term for "decking" or riding on top of a train.

Jungle. Hobo camp.

Jungle buzzard. Man who eats the food left in the jungles or begs off hoboes.

Keister. Suitcase.

Kelly stick. A device to aid in washing clothes and boiling up; a tin can with holes was placed at the end of a stick, immersed in soapy water, and pounded up and down on the clothes.

Kip. To sleep.

Knobhead. Mule.

Ky wah. Hobo pitchman who sold such items as jewelry, pens, and novelties.

Library birds. Unemployed men who lounge in libraries for shelter.

Lighthouse. One who has a knack for recognizing plainclothes detectives on sight.

Lizzie moocher. Tramp who panhandles food and gas in a car.

Lousy Anna. Less than affectionate title for Louisiana, a state less than hospitable to hoboes.

Lump. Handout.

Main stem. Main street of a city or neighborhood.

Making a riffle. Begging money.

Makins. Bull Durham or other tobacco.

Manifest. Fast freight.

Mark. Hobo sign; a person or place willing to give food or money.

Meg. Penny.

Milk and Honey route. Named for railroads in Utah that traversed Morman territory; Mormons were generally very generous to hoboes.

Minister's face. Pig's head served in cheap restaurants.

Mission stiff. Man whose profession is getting saved and, with it, free flops and food.

Moll buzzer. One who specializes in begging from women.

Monicker. Pretended name or nickname.

Moocher. Professional beggar.

Mop Mary. Scrubwoman.

Mop stick. Barfly in cheap saloon.

Mule. Corn alcohol.

Mulligan. A stew of vegetables and perhaps meat or fish.

Munies. Municipal lodging houses.

Mushfaker, mushfakir. Itinerant umbrella mender.

Navy. Cigar end.

Nickel flop. All-night movie house.

Obie. Post office.

Packing mustard. Hod carrying.

Pearl diver. Dishwasher.

Peatman, peterman. Safe-blower.

Peddler. Local or slow freight.

Pling. To beg.

Plough jockey. Farmer.

Pogey. Almshouse; workhouse.

Poke. Wallet.

Poodle. Town marshal.

Possum belly. Riding the deck of a passenger coach.

Pound the ear. To sleep.

Privates. Private dwellings.

Prushin. A young boy on the road.

Pull a pin. To quit.

Punk. Bread; a kid hobo.

Push. A road gang.

Rattler. Train.

Red eye. Whiskey.

Reefer. Refrigerator; refrigerator car.

Rot gut. Bad liquor.

Saddle blankets. Hot cakes.

Sally, Sally Ann. Salvation Army.

Salve. Butter; a bribe given to a trainman for a ride.

Sand. Sugar.

Scenery bum. A young tramp on the move for the pleasure of it.

Scissorbill. One who doesn't believe in organizing or joining labor unions; an ignorant person.

Set down. Full meal inside.

Sewer hog. Ditch digger.

Shack. Brakeman.

Shack fever. Tired, sleepy, dopey feeling.

Shine. Black man.

Shuffler. Jobless worker.

Side-door pullman. Boxcar.

Skinner. Mule driver.

Sky pilot. Mission-house minister.

Slave market. Employment agency.

Slides. Shoes.

Smoke wagon. Pistol.

Snake. Railroad switchman.

Snipes. Cigarette or cigar butts rescued from ground or gutter.

Sniping. Stealing.

Spear. To make a successful connection when mooching or begging.

Spiel. Persuasive line of talk; pitch.

Splinter belly. Carpenter.

Stake. Money to carry one over for a period of time.

Stem. Street.

Stemming. Panhandling in cities.

Stew bum. Elderly tramp wasted by rot booze.

Stiff. Any class of hobo worker: cattle stiffs, harvest stiffs, etc.

Streamlined. Traveling with little gear.

Tallow pots. Railroad firemen.

Teapot. Locomotive.

Throw the feet. To beg.

Timbers. One who sells pencils.

Town clowns. Town policemen or constables.

Trapeze artist. Rider of the rods.

Vag. All types of vagabonds: hoboes, tramps, and bums; to arrest for vagrancy.

Warthog. Trainmaster.

Weeds. Jungle.

White mule. Uncolored moonshine whiskey.

Willy. Goodwill Industries of the Methodist Church.

Wobblies, Wobs. Members of the Industrial Workers of the World (IWW).

Woodhead. Lumberjack.

Yeggs. Itinerant criminals, especially burglars and safeblowers.

Selected Bibliography

The two principal manuscript collections used in the preparation of this volume are the Papers of John J. McCook at the Antiquarian and Landmarks Society of Hartford, Connecticut, and the Papers of Ben Reitman at the University of Illinois at Chicago Circle. The McCook Papers are an extraordinary collection of letters, notebooks, survey forms, lecture notes, sermons, and drafts of papers produced by the Reverend in his long study of the tramp and hobo. The collection is available on microfilm from the Society in fourteen rolls along with a guide, *The Social Reform Papers of John James McCook*, edited by Adela Haberski French. The collection also includes the numerous photographs McCook took of his subjects, some of which appear in this book. The McCook collection provides valuable insight into the vagabond community at the turn of the century. The Reitman Papers contain superb materials on the later period, and especially the hobo fraternal organizations and the dynamics of underclass life in Chicago through the thirties.

The National Archives in Washington, D.C., has excellent material on the investigations of the U.S. Commission on Industrial Relations in Record Group 174, General Records of the Department of Labor. The Archives also has investigative files on James Eads How, Ben Reitman, and other less-known radicals in Record Group 65, Records of the Federal Bureau of Investigation, and Record Group 165, Records of the War Department General and Special Staffs, Records of the Office of the Director of Intelligence. Many of the original reports of the Commission on Industrial Relations are at the State Historical Society of Wisconsin in Madison.

The Archive of Folk Song at the Library of Congress in Washington has, as might be expected, much valuable information on hobo and Wobbly songs. Especially notable are the lyrics recorded by John O'Donnell in interviews with tramps, yeggs, and hoboes. The Archive also has a fascinating interview with Harry Kemp, the tramp poet, taken in his New York studio in January 1939 by May Swenson, long after Kemp had given up the road.

I have used extensively various editions of the *Hobo News*. The American Antiquarian Society, Worcester, Massachusetts, has the volume for 1915; the New York Public Library has several volumes on microfilm; and the National Archives has a number of issues in the FBI and military intelligence investigative files.

Several railroad magazines have much valuable material on the hobo. They include *The Railway Magazine, Railway Age,* and especially *The Railroad Gazette.* The IWW newspapers such as *Solidarity* and the *Industrial Worker* are also an excellent source on the hobo, especially for the period after 1910.

The following selected bibliography lists articles and books consulted in the preparation of this book.

Adams, Charles E. "The Real Hobo: What He Is and How He Lives." *Forum,* 33 (June 1902), 438–49.

Advisory Social Service Committee of the Municipal Lodging House. *The Men We Lodge: A Report to the Commissioner of Public Charities.* New York: New York Advisory Social Service Committee, 1915.

"All About the Entity of the 'Ego' Is Taught at the Hobo University." *Literary Digest,* 62 (July 12, 1919), 52.

Allsop, Kenneth. *Hard Travellin'.* New York: The New American Library, 1967.

Anderson, Nels. *The American Hobo.* Leiden: E. J. Brill, 1975.

———. "Highlights of the Migrant Problem Today." *Proceedings of the National Conference of Social Work,* 67 (1940), 109–17.

———. *The Hobo: The Sociology of the Homeless Man.* Chicago: University of Chicago Press, 1923.

———. "The Juvenile and the Tramp." *Journal of the American Institute of Criminal Law and Criminology,* 14 (August 1, 1923), 290–312.

———. *Men on the Move.* Chicago: University of Chicago Press, 1940.

———. *The Milk and Honey Route: A Handbook for Hoboes.* New York: Vanguard Press, 1931.

Anderson, Paul. "Tramping with Yeggs." *Atlantic Monthly,* 36 (December 1925), 747–55.

Ashleigh, Charles. *Rambling Kid.* Faber, 1930.

Bahr, Howard M. *Disaffiliated Man.* Toronto: University of Toronto Press, 1970.

Bailey, William A. *Bill Bailey Came Home: As a Farm Boy, as a Stowaway at the Age of Nine.* Logan, Utah: Utah State University Press, 1973.

Baker, Oliver E. *Seed Time and Harvest.* U.S. Department of Agriculture Bulletin No. 183, Washington, D.C., Government Printing Office, 1922.

Batchelor, Bronson. "The Hotel de Gink." *Independent* (January 25, 1915), 127–28.

Beck, Frank O. *Hobohemia.* Rindge, N.H.: R. R. Smith, 1956.

Benson, Benjamin. *500,000 Miles Without a Dollar.* New York, 1942.

Blatchly, Charles. "State Farm for Tramps and Vagrants." *Survey,* 24 (April 9, 1910), 87–89.

Blau, Raphael. "Magnificent Hobo." *Holiday,* 18 (December 1955), 178–85.

Botkin, B. A., and F. F. Harlow. *A Treasury of Railroad Folklore.* New York: Crown Publishers, 1953.

Brackett, Jeffrey. *The Transportation Problem in American Social Work.* New York: Russell Sage Foundation, 1936.

Brewer, W. H. "What Shall We Do With Tramps?" *New Englander,* 37 (1878), 521.

Brissenden, Paul. *The I.W.W.: A Study of American Syndicalism.* New York: Columbia University, 1920.

—————— and Emil Frankel. "The Mobility of Industrial Labor." *Political Science Quarterly,* 35 (December 1920), 566–94.

Bruère, Robert. "The Industrial Workers of the World." *Harper's Monthly Magazine,* 127 (July 1918), 250–57.

Bull, William. *Trampery: Its Causes, Present Aspects, and Some Suggested Remedies.* Boston: G. H. Ellis, 1886.

Bunce, Frank. "I've Got to Take a Chance." *Forum* 89 (February 1933), 108–12.

Carlin, Peter. "Social Outcasts: The Tramp in American Society, 1873–1910." Paper delivered at the annual meeting of the American Historical Association, New York, December 28, 1979.

Carnagey, Dale. "The World's Best Known Hobo." *American Magazine,* 78 (October 1914), 58–59.

Chaplin, Ralph. *Wobbly: The Rough-and-Tumble Story of an American Radical.* Chicago: University of Chicago Press, 1948.

"Chicago: Hobo Capital of America." *Survey,* 50 (June 1, 1923), 303–5.

Davies, William Henry. *The Adventures of Johnny Walker, Tramp.* London: Howard Baker, 1970.

——————. *The Autobiography of a Super-Tramp.* London: A. C. Fitfield, 1908.

DeCaux, Len. *Labor Radical: From the Wobblies to CIO.* Boston: Beacon Press/Unitarian Universalist Association, 1970.

"The Disappearing Tramp." *The Nation,* 84 (January 3, 1907), 5.

Douglas, William O. *Go East, Young Man.* New York: Dell Publishing Company, 1974.

Downing, Mortimer. "The Case of the Hop Pickers." *International Socialist Review,* 14 (October 1913), 210–13.

"Drawbacks of Being a Knight of the Road." *Literary Digest,* November 11, 1916, 1281–86.

Dubofsky, Melvyn. *We Shall Be All: A History of the Industrial Workers of the World.* Chicago: Quadrangle, 1969.

Duke, Donald. "The Railroad Tramp," *American Railroad Journal,* 2 (1967–8), 32–45.

Dunn, Martha. "Philosophy and Tramps." *Atlantic Monthly,* 97 (June 1906), 776–83.

Edge, William. *The Main Stem.* New York: Vanguard Press, 1927.

Elam, Samuel. "Lady Hoboes." *New Republic,* 61 (January 1, 1930), 164–69.

Etulain, Richard, ed. *Jack London on the Road: The Tramp Diary and other Hobo Writings.* Logan, Utah: Utah State University Press, 1977.

Facciolo, Jay. *The Wobs and the Bos: The IWW and the Hobo.* Unpublished masters thesis, Hunter College, 1977.

Feied, Frederick. *No Pie in the Sky.* New York: Citadel Press, 1964.

"For Hoboes: Hobo News." *Time,* May 17, 1937, 67–69.

Forbes, James. "Jockers and the Schools They Keep." *Charities* 11 (November 7, 1903), 432–36.

———. "The Tramp; or Caste in the Jungle." *Outlook,* 98 (August 19, 1911), 869–75.

Fox, R. M. "Rolling Stones." *Nineteenth Century,* 107 (June 1930), 846–54.

Garland, Hamlin. *A Son of the Middle Border.* New York: The Macmillan Company, 1917.

Garrard, G. A. "Boy Tramps and Reform Schools; A Reply to Mr. Flynt." *Century,* 51 (April 1896), 955.

"Gentle Art of Hoboing As Practiced by an Artist." *Literary Digest,* 70 (July 16, 1921), 40–43.

Goldman, Emma. *Living My Life.* New York: Alfred A. Knopf, 1931.

Gould, E. R. "How Baltimore Banished Tramps." *Forum,* 17 (1894), 497–504.

"The Great Historical Bum: An Introduction to Hobo Folklore." *Come All Ye,* October–December 1975.

Greeley, William. *Some Public and Economic Aspects of the Lumber Industry.* U.S. Department of Agriculture, Forest Service Report No. 114, Washington, D.C., Government Printing Office, 1917.

Green, Howard. " 'A Devil of a Lot of Questions': Reverend John McCook and His 1891 Tramp Survey." Paper presented at the annual meeting of the Organization of American Historians, New Orleans, April 1979.

"Guitar Solo to the Luring Freight Car." *Chicago Literary Times*, June 15, 1923.

Guthrie, Woody. *Bound For Glory*. New York: Doubleday & Co., 1943.

Gutman, Herbert. "Work, Culture, and Society in America, 1815–1919." *American Historical Review*, 78 (June 1973).

Haardt, Sara. "Jim Tully." *American Mercury*, 14 (May 1928), 82–89.

Hall, J. N. "How the Tramp Travels." *Harper's Weekly*, 36 (March 12, 1892), 255–56.

Harring, Sidney. "Class Conflict and the Suppression of Tramps in Buffalo, 1892–1894." *Law and Society Review*, 11 (Summer 1977).

Healy, T. F. "Hobo Hits the Highroad." *American Mercury*, 8 (July 1926), 334–38.

"Hobo Hegemony: Convention to Decide Among Rival Kings of Road Knights." *Literary Digest*, 123 (April 10, 1937), 10–12.

"Hoboes' Union." *Journal of Switchmen's Union of North America*, 16 (1914), 20–22.

Hofer, E. "The Tramp Problem." *Overland Monthly*, 23 (1893–4), 628.

Hoffmann, Victor. *The American Tramp, 1870–1900*. Dissertation, University of Chicago, 1953.

Holbrook, Stewart. *The Story of American Railroads*. New York: Crown Publishers, 1947.

Holt, A. E. " 'Bos." *Survey*, 60 (August 1, 1928), 456–59.

"How to Tell a Hobo from a Mission Stiff." *Survey*, 31 (March 21, 1914), 781.

Hubbard, Elbert. "Rights of Tramps." *Arena*, 9 (1893), 593–600.

Irwin, Godfrey. *American Tramp and Underworld Slang*. New York: Sears Publishing Co., 1930.

Irwin, Will. "The Floating Laborer." *Saturday Evening Post*, May 9, 1914.

"James Eads How: Portrait." *Collier's*, June 26, 1926, 16.

Jensen, Vernon. *Heritage of Conflict*. Ithaca, N.Y.: Cornell University Press, 1950.

Jury, Mark. "The Last American Romantic." *Ambassador*, 12 (March 1979), 46–52.

Kazarian, John. "The Starvation Army." *The Nation*, 136 (April 12–26, 1933).

Kemp, Harry. *Chanteys and Ballads*. New York: Brentano's, 1920.

———. "The Hobo." *New Republic*, 35 (August 22, 1923), 365–66.

————. "The Lure of the Tramp." *Independent*, 70 (June 8, 1911), 1270–71.

————. *Tramping on Life*. Garden City, N.Y.: Garden City Publishing Co., 1922.

Kenny, Raymond. "The 'Hobo Convention'." *Survey*, 26 (September 23, 1911), 862–64.

Kerouac, Jack. *On the Road*. New York: The Viking Press, 1955.

————. "The Vanishing American Hobo." *Holiday*, 27 (March 1960), 60.

Klein, Nicholas. "Hobo Lingo." *American Speech*, 1 (September 1926), 650–53.

Knibbs, Henry. *Songs of the Lost Frontier*. New York: Houghton Mifflin Company, 1930.

————. *Songs of the Outlands: Ballads of the Hoboes and Other Verses*. Boston: Houghton Mifflin Company, 1914.

Kornbluh, Joyce, ed. *Rebel Voices*. Ann Arbor: University of Michigan Press, 1964.

Kromer, Tom. *Waiting for Nothing*. New York: Alfred A. Knopf, 1935.

"Ladies of the Road." *Literary Digest*, 114 (August 13, 1932), 33.

Leavitt, Samuel. "The Tramps and the Law." *Forum*, 2 (1886), 190–200.

Lescohier, Don. *Conditions Affecting the Demand for Harvest Labor in the Wheat Belt*. U.S. Department of Agriculture, Bulletin No. 1230, Washington, D.C., Government Printing Office, 1924.

————. *Harvest Labor Problems in the Wheat Belt*. U.S. Department of Agriculture, Bulletin No. 1020, Washington, D.C., Government Printing Office, 1920.

————. "Harvesters and Hoboes in the Wheat Fields." *Survey*, 50 (August 1, 1923), 482–87.

————. *Sources of Supply and Conditions of Employment of Harvest Labor in the Wheat Belt*. U.S. Department of Agriculture, Bulletin No. 1211, Washington, D.C., Government Printing Office, 1924.

Levine, Louis. "The Development of Syndicalism in America." *Political Science Quarterly*, 28 (September 1913), 451–79.

Lewis, Orlando. "The American Tramp." *Atlantic Monthly*, 101 (June 1908), 744–53.

————. "Concerning Vagrancy." *Charities*, 21 (January 23, 1909), 713–17.

————. "Vagrancy in the United States." *Conference of Charities and Corrections, National Proceedings*, 1907, 52–77.

Livingston, Leon Ray. *The Curse of Tramp Life*. Cambridge Springs, Pa.: A-No. 1 Publishing Co., 1912.

————. *From Coast to Coast with Jack London*. Grand Rapids, Mich.: Black Letter Press, 1969.

————. *Here and There with A-No. 1.* Erie, Pa.: A-No. 1 Publishing Co., 1921.

————. *The Snare of the Road.* Erie, Pa.: A-No. 1 Publishing Co., 1916.

Loane, M. "A Woman Supertramp." *Living Age,* 268 (January 28, 1911), 253–55.

Lomax, Alan. *The Folk Songs of North America.* Garden City, N.Y.: Doubleday, 1960; reprinted Dolphin Books, 1975.

London, Jack. *The Road.* New York: The Macmillan Company, 1907.

Marsh, Benjamin. "Causes of Vagrancy and Methods of Eradication." *Annals of the American Academy of Political Science,* 23 (1903–4), 445–46.

Mathers, Michael. *Riding the Rails.* Boston: Houghton-Mifflin Company, 1973.

Maxwell, Cliff. "Daughters of the Road." *Railroad Magazine,* 26 (September 1939), 49–51.

————. "Lady Vagabonds." *Scribner's Magazine,* 85 (March 1929), 88–92.

McMurry, Donald. *Coxey's Army.* Seattle: University of Washington Press, 1968.

McPherson, James, and Miller Williams, eds. *Railroad: Trains and Train People in American Culture.* New York: Random House, 1976.

Meredith, Mamie. " 'Waddies' and 'Hoboes' of the Old West." *American Speech,* 7 (April 1932), 257–60.

Milburn, George. *The Hobo's Hornbook: A Repertory for a Gutter Jongleur.* New York: I. Washburn, 1930.

————. "Poesy in the Jungles." *American Mercury,* 20 (May 1930), 80–86.

" 'Millionaire Hobo' Is Dead." *Christian Century,* 47 (August 20, 1930), 1020.

Minehan, Thomas. *Boy and Girl Tramps of America.* New York: Farrar and Rinehart, 1934.

————. *Lonesome Road: The Way of Life of a Hobo.* Evanston, Ill.: Row, Peterson and Co., 1941.

"The Most Arrested American." *Literary Digest,* 86 (July 11, 1925), 50–55.

Mullin, Glen. *Adventures of a Scholar-Tramp.* New York and London: The Century Co., 1925.

————. "Adventures of a Scholar-Tramp." *Century,* 105 (February–March 1923), 507–15; 753–59.

Noble, C. W. "The Borderland of Trampdom." *Popular Science Monthly,* 50 (1896–7), 252–58.

Norris, Lowell. "America's Homeless Army." *Scribner's Magazine*, 93 (May 1933), 316–18.

Nylander, Towne. "The Migratory Population of the United States." *American Journal of Sociology*, 30 (September 1924), 129–53.
————. "Tramps and Hoboes." *Forum*, August 1925, 227–37.

O'Donnell, John. *Hobo Lore*. New York: WPA, 1938. Unpublished typescript in Archive of Folk Song, Library of Congress, Washington, D.C.

Otten, Alan. "End of the Line." *Wall Street Journal*, December 26, 1974.

Pager, George. "The Hobo News." *New York Folklore Quarterly*, 5 (Autumn 1949), 228–230.

Paine, Samuel. "Ditching the Hobo." *Railroad Man's Magazine*, 32 (April 1917), 529–45.

Parker, Carleton. "The California Casual and His Revolt." *Quarterly Journal of Economics*, 30 (November 1915), 110–26.
————. *The Casual Laborer and Other Essays*. New York: Harcourt, Brace & Howe, 1920.

Payne, Roger. *The Hobo Philosopher or The Philosophy of the Natural Life*. Fellowship Farm, Puente, Calif.: published by the author, 1918.

Peele, John. *From North Carolina to Southern California Without a Ticket*. Tarboro, N.C.: Edwards and Broughton Printing Co., 1907.

"The Philadelphia Tramp Conference." *Charities*, 11 (November 28, 1903), 514–15.

Pinkerton, Allan. *Strikers, Communists, Tramps, and Detectives*. New York: G. W. Carleton & Co., 1878.

Preston, William. "Shall This Be All? U.S. Historians Versus William D. Haywood *Et Al.*," *Labor History*, 12 (1971), 435–71.

Reckless, Walter. "Why Women Become Hoboes." *American Mercury*, 31 (February 1934), 175–80.

Ringenbach, Paul. *Tramps and Reformers, 1873–1916: The Discovery of Unemployment in New York*. Westport, Conn.: Greenwood Press, 1973.

Rood, H. E. "Tramp Problem: A Remedy." *Forum*, 25 (March 1898), 90–94.

St. John, Vincent. *The I.W.W.* Chicago: I.W.W., 1919.

Samolar, Charlie. "The Argot of the Vagabond." *American Speech*, 2 (1927), 385–92.

Saroyan, William. "Portrait of a Bum." *Overland Monthly*, 86 (December 1928), 421, 424.

Saul, Vernon. "The Vocabulary of Bums." *American Speech*, 4 (June 1929), 337–46.

Schockman, Carl. *We Turned Hobo*. Columbus: F. J. Heer Printing Co., 1937.

Seeger, Pete. *The Incompleat Folksinger*. New York: Simon & Schuster, 1972.

Seelye, John. "The American Tramp: A Version of the Picaresque." *American Quarterly*, 15 (Winter 1963), 535–53.

Service, Robert. *Collected Poems of Robert Service*. New York: Dodd, Mead, & Co., 1921.

Sister of the Road: The Autobiography of Box-Car Bertha, As Told to Dr. Ben L. Reitman. New York: Sheridan House, 1937.

Solenberger, Alice. *One Thousand Homeless Men*. New York: Charities Publication Committee, 1911.

"The South Calling a Halt on Tramps." *Survey*, 35 (February 5, 1916), 534.

Speek, Peter A. "The Psychology of Floating Workers." *Annals of the American Academy of Political and Social Science*, 69 (January 1917), 72–78.

Spence, Clark. "Knights of the Fast Freight." *American Heritage* (August 1976), 50–57.

———. "Knights of the Tie and Rail—Tramps and Hoboes in the West." *Western Historical Quarterly*, 2 (January 1971), 5–19.

Spielmann, Peter. "Hobos." *Penthouse*, 10 (May 1979), 138–45.

Stegner, Wallace. "Depression Pop." *Esquire*, 84 (September 1975), 79–83.

Stessin, Lawrence. "That Vanishing American: The Hobo." *New York Times Magazine*, August 18, 1940.

Stevens, James. "The Hobo's Apology." *Century Magazine*, 109 (February 1925), 464–72.

Sutherland, Edwin, and Harvey J. Locke. *Twenty Thousand Homeless Men*. Chicago and Philadelphia: J. B. Lippincott Co., 1936.

Swift, Morrison. "Tramps as Human Beings." *Outlook*, 52 (August 31, 1895), 342–43.

Taft, Philip. "The I.W.W. in the Grain Belt." *Labor History*, 1 (Winter 1960), 53–67.

Tascheraud, Henri. "The Art of Bumming a Meal." *American Mercury*, 5 (June 1925), 183–87.

Terkel, Studs. *Hard Times: An Oral History of the Great Depression*. New York: Avon Books, 1971.

Thanet, Octave. "The Tramp in Four Centuries." *Lippincott's Magazine*, 23 (1878–9), 565–74.

"This Is a Primer for Hobo 'Gaycats'." *Life*, October 4, 1937, 14–17.

Tugwell, Rexford. "The Casual of the Woods." *Survey*, 44 (July 3, 1920), 472–74.

Tully, Jim. *Beggars of Life*. Garden City, N.Y.: Garden City Publishing Co., 1924.

————. "Bull Horrors." *American Mercury*, 12 (October 1927), 144–50.

————. "The Lion-Tamer." *American Mercury*, 6 (October 1925), 142–46.

————. "Thieves and Vagabonds." *American Mercury*, 14 (May 1928), 18–24.

U.S. Commission on Industrial Relations. *Industrial Relations: Final Report and Testimony*. 64th Congress, 1st Session, Senate Document 415, Washington, D.C., Government Printing Office, 1916.

Van Swol, Erwin. "The Hoboes' Secret Code." *Coronet*, 48 (August 1960), 35–38.

Whitaker, Percy. "Fruit Tramps." *Century Magazine*, 117 (March 1929), 599–606.

Willard, Josiah Flynt. "Children of the Road." *Atlantic Monthly*, 77 (January 1896), 58–71.

————. "How Men Become Tramps." *Century Magazine*, 50 (October 1895), 941–45.

————. *My Life*. New York: The Outing Publishing Co., 1908.

————. "Old Boston Mary." *Atlantic*, 74 (September 1894), 318–25.

————. "The Tramp at Home." *Century Magazine*, 47 (February 1894), 517–26.

————. *Tramping With Tramps*. Montclair, N.J.: Patterson Smith Publishing Corp., 1972.

————. "Tramps and the Railroads." *Century Magazine*, 58 (June 1899), 258–66.

Wilson, Edmund. "Political Headquarters." *New Republic*, 65 (November 19, 1930), 15–16.

Witten, George. "The Open Road." *Century Magazine*, 115 (January 1928), 351–61.

————. *Outlaw Trails*. New York: Minton, Balch and Co., 1929.

Woehlke, Walter. "The Porterhouse Heaven and the Hobo." *Technical World Magazine*, 31 (August 1914), 808–13, 938.

Worth, Cedric. "The Brotherhood of Man." *North American Review*, 227 (April 1929), 487–92.

Wyckoff, Walter. *A Day with a Tramp and Other Days*. New York: Scribner's Sons, 1906.